FOR DOYLE, MY MUSE

Table of Contents

AUTHOR'S NOTE

Dear Reader:

As you read *The Blossoming of Women*, we suggest you have a personal journal at hand to jot down your feelings regarding the content in this book and that you write out your responses to the suggested "Reflections on My Journey from Older to Elder" at the end of each chapter. The ideas contained in these chapters are designed to help you ponder and record your own passage from older to elder.

Enjoy the process!

Karen Roberts

FOREWORD

In this compelling and transformational book, author Karen Roberts captures and highlights a trend in our society today that has mainly gone unnoticed—the contributions of "older" women in their sixties, seventies, and even eighties. These are the women that she calls "elders." They are past retirement age, no longer raising their families or caring for aged parents. They are usually also widowed or divorced. They are often answering a call that comes to them unexpectedly, out of the blue, like caring for homeless women on the street.

What makes this book both timely and transformational is that it invites all of us "old" readers to become elders and suggests a path for doing so. We may need first to acknowledge and experience some "paths of darkness" that can come upon us as we age—both of spirit and psyche—and grief. Roberts lays out practices for transformation taken from Jungian psychology, Sufism, and Hinduism. All that frees us up to let our intuition and creativity take over and to follow our dreams. As suggested in the title, this is a workbook. At the end of each chapter, helpful questions can clarify our wants and help us on our journey to becoming an elder.

Karen Roberts is a person of courage, resilience, and creativity, all the qualities that she is encouraging us readers to develop on our paths to becoming elders. In many ways, her journey resembles what she was writing about. After college, she worked on Wall Street and married a doctor, who it turned out was bipolar. They divorced, and she moved to Santa Barbara, California, where she met a fashion designer, Joel. She later bought a twenty-acre ranch in Solvang. She and Joel spent ten years running the ranch, relishing the freedom of living with nature, and being near her horse.

Karen was studying for her PhD and had only her dissertation left. It was to be about the stages of spiritual growth in women. She dropped her dissertation in favor of writing this book. One of the motivating factors was having multiple sclerosis and admitting that her aging would be especially challenging. The other was that her mother became an alcoholic in her old age. Karen wanted to write about women who chose another route than her mother, becoming elders instead.

Karen was diagnosed with MS before there were treatments from traditional Western medicine, so she sought treatments from Eastern and indigenous peoples. She immersed herself in a program of Native American study rituals, including taking ayahuasca, a medicinal herb from Peru, a sacred medicine of the tribes there. She spent a year with the leader and became close with other students in the group, including women. It was the first time that she had reached out to women. It changed her life. She had always avoided women, looking at them as enemies.

So much of what Karen has written resonates with me. I am in my eighties. In my sixties, I earned my doctorate in couple and family therapy and got divorced. I continued in my private practice as a couple and family therapist. One morning in late August, a professor in my doctoral program called to say that the person who was to teach family systems theory in a master's program at a local graduate school unexpectedly had to drop out. The course was to start in two weeks. Would I be willing to take it on? Without hesitation, I said, "Yes!" I hung up in astonishment and disbelief. I was typically someone cautious, wanting to be fully prepared for anything I did. All I could think was that this willingness to go for it must be the result of a weeklong personal development workshop I had just attended. In the morning run, in our shares, we were encouraged not to hold back but push past our fears and self-imposed limits.

I loved teaching and did it for several years until another opportunity presented itself. I was invited to be a "trainer" in a program called More to Life, leading personal development weekends. I would be in front of a room with twenty to forty participants, doing therapeutic work with them when they stood to share. It often required confrontation. It also involved travel because the weekends were held around the States, in the UK, South Africa, and New Zealand. Both teaching and training were a far cry from being a therapist in private practice, seeing clients in my office, and doing a lot of listening. It's as if I finally found my voice and loved doing what I never imagined I would do. I became an elder.

Anne Chalfont Brown
January 2023

INTRODUCTION

W ho are the women who shine their brightest in their twilight years? Who stand in the vanguard at an age when most have chosen to retreat from society? What motivates these women to seek new paths? What enkindles their sense of purpose? These questions have become increasingly relevant and persistent in my life as I move into my seventh decade.

Late life sometimes presents an identity crisis when there are few compelling societal roles for women who must answer a very personal call, an inner call, to find direction. Some identify this as a spiritual calling or a creative urge; for others it's a desire to seek deeper skills in an established field of work. To be of service is a common refrain.

A sense of loss often surrounds this crisis of identity, a woman's role in the family or workforce fades, and an awareness of mortality looms. Self-help books to aid the struggling female at this stage are missing from the shelves. She may feel abandoned by her friends and family alike as she enters a dark night of the soul. It is a solitary path. How long will it take? Will she abandon the calling?

I have found the women who excel in their later years, are beyond retirement age, well past the years of childbearing, and thriving in unconventional roles. They carry an inspiration to continue, to perfect previous capacities or to start anew, sometimes on a creative path only dreamed of before. What enables these women to find the energy to choose a more challenging direction rather than accept the identity of an aging woman who simply watches life pass by?

The year 2017 was an exciting time for women in America. The #MeToo movement brought a new awareness of female strength and solidarity. In the rest of the world, women were gaining political presence: in Great Britain, Germany, and New Zealand, they held national leadership positions. The second and third waves of feminism in America contributed greater recognition for the talents of younger women in certain socio-economic classes and for Black women for the first time, but many weren't reached. Mothers still waited for childcare while they home-schooled their children during the COVID-19 pandemic and for equal pay across the economic spectrum.

For the most part, appreciation for the contributions made by older women to society still has not occurred. In the United States, we see the older female as one who has lost her physical attractiveness or allure as a femme fatale. In my experience, the older woman is generally unseen and resented as being needy and useless. She may remain the mother until the children leave home, and then she is the warden of an empty nest; her purpose, as designated by cultural expectations, now finished. If she chooses to retire, she must relinquish her achievements in the workforce and her rank as a financial provider. There is no post-retirement role.

In other cultures, indigenous cultures especially, roles are assigned to each age and stage; tribal rituals grant new identities. Respect is given to older individuals as the ones of wisdom, the storytellers, who keep the memories of what happened before. They are considered elders: tribal gifts. In contemporary America, by contrast, older members are often forgotten or placed in retirement homes.

Modern American culture ignores the older female despite the extraordinary abilities she often possesses to assist her fellows. She may have extra powers to understand the depth of another's psychological barriers and gifts, to assist in the release of creative and interpersonal abilities, or to guide in spiritual development. She may be a great soul who brings unity to a broken community or a broken heart, and she may help to heal the split between humankind and nature.

Some women in their sixties and seventies and into their eighties experience an inspiration to start anew. At seventy-three years of age, I am one of these women who wish to choose the more challenging path rather than "turn away." I believe I have a contribution to make at this time that will be more personal and impactful than in my earlier years. I feel steadier, more confident, and, in a way, more optimistic in how I can serve. I want to give more and allow the lessons I have learned to bring me closer to others while expanding my consciousness.

The mission of this book is to explore the path from older to elder. In the following chapters, I will share attitudes and perspectives, as well as theories and research on aging that may surprise you, and I hope invigorate you to believe there is more ahead. You are at the crossroads of what can be an extraordinary new beginning in your life. I will also share the stories of a select group of women in their later lives who are unique in their capabilities to give to their communities, but their paths were not straight or easy. Once I started seeking older women to interview, I encountered them in different ways, but most came through word-of-mouth. This was a beautiful testament that when we avail ourselves of what is around us, we find the way as if being guided and break into new passions.

The interviewees did not readily share their journeys until I gave them the background of this project and my intention to create a workbook. Only then did they break out of their private shells in the hopes of helping. I believe their stories are not just about growing old and finding one's voice and inner wisdom but also about how to face challenges and life crises at any stage. They all demonstrate incredible resilience and a newfound purpose after facing their times of chaos. On a final note, although I did not interview Jane Goodall, she has written extensively about her work and her life and is a woman and an elder I greatly admire. I believe we can learn from her determination and accomplishments.

Because I have created this to be a workbook to encourage and support you in your own self-discovery, a selection of questions accompanies each chapter. As you tune inwards, perhaps exploring some of the practices for transformation I describe, take a moment to ask your "voice within" the questions I propose. It is my hope that these questions and my writing can be a resource for older women who sense the excitement of renewed purpose. May the answers that come light your way. I truly believe aging can be so much more than the gradual decline toward death.

Chapter One

OLDER OR ELDER

Louise Erdrich, who grew up in North Dakota, has a unique closeness to the land and the tribal people of her upbringing. Her mother was part Ojibwa and part French. Erdrich told the *AARP Bulletin*, "The Ojibwa people call old people 'wisdom keepers.' They are treasures. They're also the funniest people in the community. The elders have the freedom to tease anybody." This observation demonstrates what I believe is especially true for women as we age: we become the keepers of wisdom.

What is the difference between an "older" and an "elder" woman? Older refers to those who age, adding years to their lives, but no longer have eyes to see the needs or beauty of others. An older woman may be so concerned with herself, demanding attention and success even in her final years, that she does not look beyond herself except to compare and compete. This type of female carries the myth of Narcissus regardless of age. She remains with her mirror of self and is not able to sink into a deeper level of relationship. Older women who have not developed spiritually through a late-life identity crisis remain in the handcuffs of their egos. Their growth toward relationship either with others or with God is hampered. Elders, I propose, are those who have undergone transformation after a crisis, refusing to allow egos or stereotypes to block their growth.

The transformation from older to elder requires an ability to turn away from the many distractions of modern culture, distractions that are deeply embedded in beliefs about our uselessness in old age. The expectations of old age in modern culture keep a person, a female in particular, from moving into a new identity. A Western attitude assumes respect for a woman solely based on youth. Older women wither away from self-criticism, grieving loss of beauty, family, or career. Lacking cultural appreciation for age and the wisdom that comes from aging, older people fail to appreciate themselves. This is an unretractable loss for us all. I believe you become an elder when you accept your age with appreciation and honor your responsibility to others. When you take on a role as artist or teacher, healer, or spiritual guide to assist those in your community to develop their gifts, you are an elder.

According to Erik Erikson, one of the most well-known psychoanalysts of the twentieth century, there are eight stages of psychosocial development, and each stage requires a crisis. Human development ends in ego-integrity, which is the integration of the accomplishments from previous stages. The "accomplishments" are levels of independence characterized by increased identity-building and autonomy. The final accomplishment of integrity and wisdom is not guaranteed by age but by successful transitions over one's lifetime. Positive resolution of each stage may allow wisdom in old age; however, most of us are broken by the climb up the ladder and feel only despair and disappointment at the end of life. Erickson characterizes this distress as a failure to resolve the challenges of each stage and to integrate the character-building opportunities.

While Erikson's model provides a useful understanding of many aspects of human development across the lifespan, it does not consider how or why women often show increased affinity for the dimension of oneness, for unity, in late life; a perspective central to this book and first proposed by researchers at the Stone Center for Developmental Services and Studies at Wellesley College. Mutual empathy and intuition, as theorized by Janet Surrey, research associate at the center, lead to "zest and vitality emerging from connection." Surrey refutes traditional models that consider human development to be the maturation of independence and autonomy and proposes that for women, maturation of ability occurs through connection and growth-fostering relationships.

If men achieve a more defined sense of self through separation and competitive ability, women grow by means of relational affinity and empathy. In some respects, the very goal of aging diverges between men and women. Following Erikson's model, maturation is the process of becoming more self-reliant and independent; however, there is significant shortsightedness in the presumption that anyone can exist without support from others. Jean Miller, director of education at the Stone Center, provides a powerful reconsideration of aging when she questions the traditional theory that development of the self is attained through a series of painful crises by which the individual accomplishes a sequence of allegedly essential separations from others, thereby achieving individuation. "Few men ever attain such self-sufficiency, as every woman knows. They are usually supported by wives, mistresses, mothers, secretaries, nurses and other women." We all live within a network of relationships, dependent on support from others. When we are aware of these relationships, we act with empathy, becoming more sensitive individuals who respond to others and experience the empowering energy of connection.

For Native Americans, respecting the land and the wisdom it gives them is similar to the mutuality sought by females. Growth in connection is a goal honored by tribal people whose community is all-important and for whom the natural world is viewed as a spiritual entity, their mother and Great Spirit. Poet laureate Joy Harjo who was raised on a reservation, writes of loss, a fall from grace, even among her people of the Muscogee (Creek) tribe, when this connection is broken:

In the legend are instructions on the language of the land,

how it was we forgot to acknowledge the gift,

as if we were not in it or of it.

Take note of the proliferation of supermarkets and malls,

the altars of money.

They best describe the detour from grace.

(Joy Harjo, "A Map to the Next World")

Humankind is losing its sense of divinity, and the information glut of modernity is as devastating to the soul as supermarkets and malls. In his book *What Are Old People For?* gerontologist William Thomas shares the wealth elders can contribute as storytellers to restore the human spirit. As the richly endowed, they offer more than expertise and information; they blend it and enrich it with wisdom for the purpose of sharing stories. Stories come to life in the moment of their telling, enrich the listener, and enhance the cultural memory. The sharing of stories instills respect for the land along with all its living creatures. As younger generations are reminded of the blessings of the world around them, of the magic that resides behind the bushes and under the rocks, they are pulled from the technologies of games and social media back to the endless awe of nature's bounty. The real-life wisdom of elders can pull generations of youth back from the abyss of their feelings of not belonging.

Elders have always made important contributions to the young in their families and their communities. Elder councils in tribal societies provide a balancing perspective to consider the long-term results, always considering the effects on seven generations beyond themselves. Elders in the Western world currently hold power in their numbers to alter the direction of culture and political reality to ensure an enduring, abundant world. They can be like the elder councils of tribes, directing us toward greater health. Thomas says that "the amount of life experiences they can bring to bear on the important problems that face our society is huge and will only grow as the decades pass. We are living in an era of enormous wealth and possibility and should be welcoming the age boom with cries of joy from every rooftop."

Whether we look for the influence of elders as a political movement or as individuals, we need to see the richness. Older women, females still bound by earlier life values, are often judgmental of those who have broken away from the expectations of others; they are not open to beginning again. The unusual choices that many elders make in the last part of their lives are not "attractive." To be drawn to caring for the homeless on our streets or apes in Africa or to join hospice to sing to the dying requires a movement from within and the open arms of universal love. Elders, like the women you will meet later in this book, follow a desire from deep inside to care for others, to heal like the mythical Chiron.

Women who fail to respond to the transformational challenge presented in late life miss the magic of a new beginning. These are the ones we call older, hanging onto the same old identity and doing the same old imitation of their former selves. Those who follow one of the paths of transformation described in the following chapters find renewal and answers to the questions of "What am I going to do with myself?" and "What is this time for?" The gift of additional decades of life does have meaning in giving us an opportunity to discover our life purpose, the unique reason we were created. We are each one-of-a-kind and have our own stories to tell.

Reflections on My Journey
from Older to Elder

1. Describe in a few sentences what you understand as the differences between growing older and becoming an elder. How does this awareness change your thinking about your aging?

2. Can you identify an individual you know who emulates the kind of person you hope to be when you reach old age?

3. What are your fears about growing old?

4. Identify the life achievements of which you are most proud. What is missing from this list? Can you see a dream you still wish to fulfill?

5. What distractions or perceived duties in your life are stopping you from moving on? What images of yourself are holding you back?

Now you are moving into being an elder.

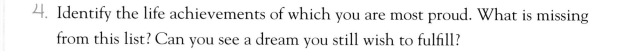

Chapter Two

PATHS OUT OF DARKNESS

A woman in the second half of her life loses the attributes of youthful attraction and reproductive fertility and the personas of responsibility gained in middle age as mother or corporate leader. Close relationships are often inalterably disrupted by sickness or the loss of a spouse from death or divorce. The feelings of powerlessness and fear that accompany these physical and emotional challenges can be devastating. Women frequently internalize the assaults of ageism that tell them they can't or that they shouldn't even try. A weakening of her will and a steady decline may be her response, especially if she cannot hear the inner voices of hope and direction.

Jungian psychoanalyst and author James Hollis writes in his book *Finding Meaning in the Second Half of Life*:

"The second half of life presents a rich possibility for spiritual enlargement, for we are never going to have greater powers of choice, never have more lessons of history from which to learn, and never possess more emotional resilience, more insight into what works for us and what does not, or a deeper, sometimes more desperate, conviction of the importance of getting our lives back."

These possibilities in late life are not given but earned from a lifetime of lessons and insight. There is no reason to surrender or fade away at a time when your hands are full of an abundance of gifts. To see this period for what it can be, a time of expansion in our lives, is a radical reconsideration of what it means to grow old. The identity crisis usually refers to a struggle in younger years, and only in recent decades is the term applied to a reality for a senior citizen. This crisis, however, is often the trigger for opening the war chest of potentials for future self-realization. Being lost in a darkness of pain or meaninglessness may, in fact, bring you to the cusp of getting your life back.

When I was uprooted by a late-life identity crisis, I found myself without a family role model to follow. Although my mother was flourishing in her duties as a social hostess, alcohol was a painful part of that role, and my grandmother was a single parent and nurse during the war who had left her family to work at Pearl Harbor. Both were females caught in traditional roles and experiences different from mine. Neither had the luxury of time to seek relationships with their daughters nor a spiritual path separate from the orthodox one given to them.

The inner work of later life has long been appreciated in Eastern cultures and among indigenous peoples worldwide. America and Europe, however, have failed to grant what I would describe as a "philosophy of aging" for women. After the release from outer roles, what is a woman to do? With few guides, she will inevitably feel bereft. Today, awareness is growing that she may have another opportunity for personal and spiritual development. A redefinition of aging is on the horizon but with few words of wisdom to help. Despair marks the elder years for many; however, the manner of coping with these uncertainties is not etched in some stone of aging. There is a very real opportunity to live again.

After I was diagnosed in middle age with multiple sclerosis, I searched for healing practices in traditions beyond my Western mindset. My experiences with Sufism and Shamanism helped me feel whole again and informed an attitude and perspective on aging. Sufism is about changing consciousness. Whirling and ecstatic dance are a form of meditation or prayer for Sufis. To the observer, we are swaying and gyrating bodies, but it goes much deeper than movement. I still remember how some participants fell in joy, others in tears, while a few sat in calm meditation. Through all this, we were accomplishing the chosen way: separating our spirits from the control of mind and body. And we were doing it together as 120 women and five men.

Although neurologists were telling me there was no cure, the drumming rhythm brought about another dimension of existence beyond the reality of my body, which was having a medical crisis. I still can feel the intricate waves of dreamlike joy as all negative thoughts, problems, and tension left my mind and body. In the desert those summers with my Sufi master and the other students, I was shown another world, the world of spirit, separate from the expectations and demands of everyday life in competitive America. I was given a new life where only the stars and the music spoke to me. There was no inner voice reminding me of my role.

Dropping the values for success is "unnatural" and contrary to a lifetime of being trained to excel. Most of us come of age in school, whether public or private, which trains us to be self-critical. As we age, we continue to hold these judgments, though we learn to hide them even from ourselves. A late-life identity crisis can break open our armor to the truth hidden behind a lifetime of pretense. Crises can serve us.

Later, when I sought healing from Native American Shamanism, I was told the sacred medicine of ayahuasca would take me through a dark tunnel, frightening at first, like the tunnel of final transformation. During my ayahuasca trip to the other world, I reached out to the women in our group. For forty years, I had frowned on women, not identified with them or trusted them, and now I was seeking solace from them. Previously I had not chosen the path of motherhood and thus felt I didn't relate to their concerns. This pivotal experience opened me to the world I now write about—the world of female elders. I had to shed my stereotypes and disregard for the feminine even to imagine and be receptive to the idea of female elders and of aging as an empowering act.

The sacred medicine of ayahuasca did it for me. It broke through my barriers of judgment and self-criticism. From my perspective, females typically giggled and plotted and told tales about others that hurt and belittled. I had learned how to dress up and behave with the gestures of a female but certainly couldn't find any cause to want to be like them in any other way. Despite my lifetime of learning to distrust other women, I was drawn to their natural supportiveness and embrace as I experienced the healing of aya-huasca. Although I didn't personally know her, I allowed one participant to hold me as a mother would a child. My years on Wall Street peeled away in an instant. With sacred medicine, I discovered that the challenging education and experience I had pursued to earn a career as a stock analyst and director of research were of no relevance in the new realm of consciousness. I suddenly understood a deep belonging that my life had lacked.

These experiences of changed consciousness were gifts after many dark days and nights of not knowing the possibilities of understanding myself and joining others with-out judgment. In her book *Aging from the Inside Out*, Connie Zweig terms life disruptions as the divine messengers of age. Unfortunately, we are not shown how to heed the mes-sengers or given guides for transitional times in later years. Preachers and doctors advise us to follow the written commandments of a holy life and healthy living. There is no map to finding meaning or a passion again. I choose to view our stage of life between retirement and frail old age as an open, undefined period. We can shift away from previ-ous identities and begin to live from a new center of purpose, but often only after we go through a period of fog or liminality. We may need to allow ourselves a period of grief as we let go of our past. Whether we must endure personal illness, loss of family as children move away, loss of meaning as employment changes, or loss of a beloved partner, we are being tossed into a turbulent sea.

Any loss can be a divine messenger if we are brave enough to listen. Fear is sometimes the only obstacle blocking the path to reentry to a new self, a new world. Loss can launch us down a variety of difficult paths. Depending on the life challenges you are facing, one of the paths will resonate more than the others and will help you experience the aging process as transformative.

FIRST PATH OF DARKNESS - THE SPIRITUAL

Dark night of the soul is often used in reference to the period of doubt expressed by mystics. Having forsaken the controls of church hierarchy, mystics found themselves in a forest with no clear way, no stories of previous solitary figures finding the spiritual foods to survive, let alone thrive. When we are lost or feel forsaken, we have entered a dark night of the soul.

In the sixteenth century, St. Teresa of Avila was both mystic and reformer of herself and the church, dedicated to purification and discipline. Her ongoing conversion was an arduous lifelong struggle. She expressed her own ecstatic experiences in numerous writings, but the essence is in this poem:

I have surrendered and given my all,
and the trade I have made is such
that my Beloved is all for me,
and I am all for my Beloved.

When the sweet Hunter shot me
and left me vanquished
in the arms of love,
my soul, in falling,
was gaining its new life.
Such is the trade I have made,
that my Beloved is all for me
and I am all for my Beloved.

(St. Teresa of Avila, "I Have Surrendered and Given my All")

St. John of the Cross, also a mystic of the Middle Ages, wrote, "Although this happy night brings darkness to the spirit, it does so only to give it light in everything; and that, although it humbles it and makes it miserable, it does so only to exalt it and to raise it up."

Both Teresa and John of the Cross endured hardships unimaginable in modern times of comfort and excess; they were cut off from their church in their final days, only to be sainted after death. Both wrote extensively to God of their struggles, and their experiences of feeling forsaken. In their inner craving to unite with the divine, the mystics suffered not only their longing for God but also an anger at the impossibility of being united; St. John whipped himself to know the suffering of Christ more intimately.

Our hardships are not as harsh as those of the great mystics, but our period of doubt and hopelessness can be as dark. When we accept that what has occurred in our lives may have caused suffering and perhaps forces us to distrust or to make choices we regret, we can strive again with fresh eyes. Although speaking of the spiritual path, I believe Father Thomas Keating encourages a deeper engagement with the self and others similar to what we can discover as we age. As we emerge from this period of redefinition into the light, we experience a sense of union, a "growing sense of equality with other humans, accountability for the care and preservation of the earth and its living and inorganic resources… Respect for others diminishes the drive to dominate and control. Cooperation replaces unbridled competition. Harmony replaces rigid value systems. Negotiating replaces exclusive self-interest …"

In writing of spiritual stages, Harry Moody and David Carroll describe the first stage as the crossroads in which an individual decides whether or not to take the initial step acknowledging the need to proceed on a spiritual path. Then the individual journeys into darkness and along a downward spiral into sadness, depression, or anguish. The reasons for not taking this first step are many, but essentially, we are too frightened to take a leap of faith or dread the shame of looking like a fool. Knowing the present pain is easier than searching for what may be worse. If we begin to shed our well-structured outer self, we must allow a disintegration of all that we have built our lives for, not only the material benefits but also the appearance of being stalwart and brave or beautiful in our designer dress. We must reveal our vulnerability.

We may also fear becoming lost because our spiritual guide is vague or completely missing from our lives. If we have followed a spiritual path, desiring a closer communion with the divine, we may now feel an absence, a sense of abandonment from the divine. The darkness may last for days or years as we await a voice or a touch to tell us to continue this path of seeking. Allowing the ego to dwindle, allowing the selves we have depended on through a lifetime to let go of control, is a humbling task. Emily Dickinson wrote:

"The struggle of heart and the struggle of mind
Is the struggle to learn to let go."

As one allows or gives up the struggle of denial, the spiritual cave of darkness may cause a shedding of all worldly accomplishments and achievements. The timeless questions of "Who am I?" and "What may I become in the future?" may be replaced with a new sense of energy and purpose without the existential doubt. Some draw similarities between a female giving birth; a period of darkness, doubting, fearfulness, waiting, waiting for the first breath in the infant child.

A mystic yearns for a closeness with a God who eludes her. She is continuously in a dance with a disappearing lover, in anguish for an unattainable longed-for other. Her light at the end of an unknowable time may be a glimpse or a glorious awakening. The modern spiritual seeker may go through periods of yearning and anguish like the mystics of the Middle Ages. Moving through a field of the unknown or entering a dark cave of fear describes the passage.

SECOND PATH OF DARKNESS - THE PSYCHE

Sigmund Freud and Carl Jung, modern guides to the psyche, have filled volumes with their psychological concepts. I will not attempt to condense their work but introduce a final container – the metaphor of alchemy. Alchemy is an ancient process of the secret ritualized steps of turning lead into gold. The basic ingredients were put in a hermetically sealed container and placed over a fire. In Jungian analysis, the cooking process is metaphorically similar to the transformation process. Similarly, gold is equivalent to insight. Further developing this metaphor in the modern therapeutic setting, the analyst is the vessel holding the energy.

In addition to the metaphorical relationship between the materials of alchemy and those of analysis, Jung also adopted three stages of the alchemical process, which correspond to phases of analysis: blackness, whitening, and reddening. Blackness is the stage of confusion and chaos and confrontation with shadow. Whitening involves purification or insight, and the final stage of reddening, or search for the gold, is the reunification of body and soul in analysis.

Dealing with the shadow is the path of darkness where the individual confronts personal obstacles, whether an inner critic or fear or guilt or whatever causes self-doubt to arise to stop her from accepting the call. Denial is the primary response of those whose shadows are in control. Suffering in confusion and doubt frequently delays or blocks the individual from moving forward. However, in the words of Jungian analyst Monika Wikman, "Crisis and pain often catalyze a genuine heartfelt attempt to reach toward the mysteries. In the grip of pain, we more readily reach through the veils of forgetfulness and wiles of the shadow attitudes that block the heart path."

Wikman warns, "Authentic relationship with darkness and unknowing usually brings about a shamanic death (the alchemical *nigredo)*. It is not for the fainthearted, and it is way beyond the ego's fantasies, attachments or ideas of grandeur. It includes experiences of 'hell', as well as 'heaven', as we attempt to find the optimal relationship with the flame. Jung found that a victory for the Self always included a defeat for the ego, an experience we are sure to have if seeking alchemical renewal."

Experiences of disruption and desolation are characteristics of this identity crisis, of this stage of the alchemical process, of beginning the descent into darkness. In this state of crisis, the psyche contains a fire capable of clearing the obstacles to transformation. We may know the drive as an instinct for further development or a desperate plea for discovery.

THIRD PATH OF DARKNESS - GRIEF

Loss and concomitant anger are pathways to new beginnings if the individual is able to do the inner work. The feelings of loss and betrayal are similar to those of Dr. Elisabeth Kübler-Ross's five stages of grief. From denial and anger through bargaining, we face similar psychological dramas as we age. Whether dealing with the death of a loved one or a beloved part of our life, whether personal or global, we experience the same stages of grief. The same inner work is required for an individual to move on, to release attachment to the past. The ability to be aware of sorrow and disorientation, to proceed with a life beyond, may take days or years or may never be accomplished. A new identity is waiting but not guaranteed.

Dr. Kübler-Ross studied the stages of death, first for the dying, then for the family. All those involved suffer parallel emotions of denial and anger, and both responses separate us from ourselves and from each other. The guidance of her words from decades ago gives us the tools to frame and identify our feelings today. Grief is the anguish of loss, of the ground underneath being pulled away, of seeing endless longing. We feel thrown into a world with nothing remaining from the world we had counted on, whether it's a loss of a loved one, a job, or our physical self. It feels as if we're facing the loss of all meaningful things. How can we recover?

After his stroke when he discovered he couldn't even speak, Ram Dass wrote, "I had to go beyond my intellect, into the silence of my intuitive heart. As I became more absorbed in the heart, I found it to be a place where separation disappears and knowledge gives way to wisdom."

Grief showed Dass how to appreciate silence and the deep wisdom of his intuitive heart. We each may rest in silence to find an inner gift in our grief. The story doesn't end with our loss if we search to see where the grace is hidden, if we allow a new start. The grief is setting us free; it is changing us.

Our grief may overwhelm us with sadness, making us feel hopelessly dejected and a victim, or it may fill us with anger, again causing us to feel overwhelmed. We can feel anger toward a person or circumstance we perceive as the cause of our loss when often there isn't anyone to blame. We may cry when we feel the pain of the trees being cut for timber or the deer who have lost their home in the forest because of a devastating fire. Or we can respond by seeking others working toward a solution. Both sadness and anger can lead us back to our community. Aging need not be a process that separates us in hopelessness as we deal with grief or anger, but rather one that returns us and reknits us into the social fabric. This is not a time of isolation. This is a time of extraordinary possibility.

The three paths of darkness can help guide us through a late-life stage of development. We can choose to answer the call and leap into the unknown to emerge with a unique gift, a gift of self.

REFLECTIONS ON MY JOURNEY FROM OLDER TO ELDER

1. Have you been feeling lost and disillusioned about who you are? You may be disoriented and have lost your sense of belonging because of some event. If so, what do you think the event or recent cause of this crisis might be?

2. Disorientation or life disruptions often stem from losses—loss of a loved one, your health, a job, or perhaps your children have left home, or you are questioning your faith in God. What major life changes have occurred?

3. You are in the process of dropping the self that has been your protection but is no longer effective. Are you afraid of losing your attractiveness or your ability to influence others because of a position in your career that you are giving up or have lost? How so?

4. What characteristics might you be letting go of: self-importance, self-righteousness, self-will, self-centeredness? There may also be other characteristics that have blocked you. Some women remain hidden beneath low self-esteem or a sense that they must sacrifice and not follow their dreams. Is this true for you? How has letting go of these dreams changed you or your life direction?

5. Looking back over your life, can you see experiences that helped you strip away your no-longer-useful self? Write them down.

You are at the beginning of a potential new journey.

Chapter Three

PRACTICES FOR TRANSFORMATION

How can we blossom with age and be born again? If we have spent half a lifetime building who we are, how can we choose again? Dr. Joe Dispenza wrote an entire book on *Breaking the Habit of Being Yourself*. We are given a chance at another life in our later years if we allow it. This second cycle of maturity may be seen as a letting go. We allow prior identities to fall or to be ripped away as we face the fears and expectations that have cast their shadow over our authentic selves. In this final life cycle, we are on a path to becoming who we were meant to be.

Detachment from outworn identities and dependencies is the essential process to initiation and transformation. Crisis is often the name for the beginning of this stage of maturation. It may feel as if the bedrock on which we built our identities is being whisked away. On one level, a woman who loses a reality she previously assumed as a usable identity is seeking the light of new awareness. For the Hindus, aging strips away pride, pleasures, and profit to allow the individual to seek the sacred. Hindus embrace going off into the forest and leaving behind the responsibilities of daily chores and distractions. Loss is liberation.

Being an older woman who is willing to find a new sense of self is sometimes seen as taking a forbidden path. If she allows her wisdom to guide her and chooses to follow this urging, she may find herself raising her voice to question social pillars or established norms. If she chooses to go into the darkness and gain from the transformation, she will have an immense and powerful clarity of herself. An older person who wants to be engaged in the throes of an "active" life might be considered irreverent when she is, in fact, acting on behalf of her higher self, becoming the woman she was intended to be.

In the past, we may have been given a path and a plan, but the map didn't include our soul. As doers, we achieved first in school, then in family or career. Challenges were many, and abilities were often meager as we grew through the stages of establishing our homes or careers. We are now traveling on the inner frontier, and the map no longer matches the territory we inhabit. Disruptions or crises are gifts that make us hesitate or stop on the paths we followed in our earlier years of career, family, or a combination. Our egos cannot manage anymore. If we listen, exciting possibilities will appear. We may not discover a new life, not yet, but a new dream. Maybe we will follow a new direction in a previous career or deepen the learning or aptitude of our former work. We may unearth a passion for protecting future generations and the environment or gain the insight to guide others.

We may not have the physical or financial strengths of earlier times, but we do have the wisdom of age. We have experienced nearly a lifetime. A certain courage is required to follow the calling from within, to listen to the still, small voice. Even though most prefer the safe path and not stepping into the unknown, the inner voice tells us we must dare. We are to become pilgrims without a home.

I have discovered three approaches that can guide us through the process of discovery and transformation. The first is a spiritual relationship with God or Spirit through prayer, meditation, or mindfulness. The second is a psychological practice of Jungian analysis to lead to greater consciousness. The third is accepting and recovering from grief to manifest who you want to be. In some ways, an older woman lost in a fruitless identity is seeking the light of new awareness. This is the search for personal transformation and a deeper self.

PRAYER AND MEDITATION

Father Thomas Keating said the Christian spiritual path is based on a developing trust in God. "It is trust that first allows us to take the leap in the dark, to encounter God at a deeper level of ourselves. And it is trust that guides that internal refashioning of our being, the transformation of our pain, our woundedness and unconscious motivation into the person that God intended us to be."

When we lose our divine guidance, whether from a crisis of loss or of spiritual darkness, we are invited to answer the call; we are challenged to believe in ourselves and overcome our fears.

In his book *Dark Night of the Soul*, Gerald May, MD, presents his interpretation of the dark nights of the soul shared by sixteenth-century mystics St. Teresa and John of the Cross. The dark time allows you "to see authentic attachment as leading to freedom *for* desire. The essence of all human desire is love." For mystics deep in the darkness, God was instilling a better love. Through their transformations, they were freed from their prior attachments and thus able to become completely in love with God and their neighbors. As they were relieved of a sense of separation from God, they slowly realized their union with God as an active participation *in* God. To understand this mystical, intimate co-participation with the divine, one must comprehend that God and the individual are not separate.

Finding this state of union or love is only possible after letting go and being filled with a sense of emptiness. May believes that Teresa and John relinquished their attachments of desire. In *Dark Night of the Soul*, May emphasizes that "liberation comes neither through understanding, nor through perception or image of God, but only through the total emptying of all things." The dark night of the soul is a process of liberation. The limitation of attachment is abandoned to make room for a fresh openness to love.

Our journey through darkness may guide us to an awareness of our physical body unknown to us before. Mindfulness is a traditional meditation of Buddhists and yogis that is spreading throughout Europe and America. One teacher, Willa Baker, describes the body as the conduit to integrate the head and heart. It may be experienced in visualizing an animal or person we have known in our lives that radiated spontaneous kindness. Specifically, Baker describes the practice of the natural refuge tree, a meditation that guides you to letting your attention descend to the base of your body, imagining the roots of a tree spreading from the lower spine while branches reach out from your crown. Looking above in your mind's eye, watch the branches swaying gently in the wind, whispering in the breeze. As you gaze upward through the canopy of branches, you begin to glimpse faces. "The branches of this tree are peopled with benevolent presences, those who have taught, inspired, guided, and loved you throughout your life: teachers, guides, kind relatives, loving friends and family, children, pets, buddhas, animal spirits, guides, saints, sages, angels," Baker wrote. "Some are living, some have passed on. You feel them as if they were truly present."

This meditation may not be as readily available to some as the contemplative prayer of Father Keating. If we have been raised with a familiarity of the Christian church, we may still seek prayer with God.

For those not inclined to a spiritual practice of prayer or meditation, seeking a closer relationship with the divine may be a walk in the forest. Angeles Arrien writes, "From the beauty of time we spend in nature and the mystery that we find in the sweet territory of silence, we draw a primal comfort, solace, and grace that deepen our connection to our inherent spirituality." Nature *is* the divine.

THE PSYCHE'S GOLD

If we don't follow the Christian tradition, Jungian analysis gives the alchemical ending of gold, the transmutation of lead where body, mind, and soul are unified. The psyche's journey to Jung's spirit is different from the mystic's or contemporary meditator's, wrapped as it is in dream analysis and conscious archetypal work, but the goal and realization are similar. Who are we beyond our masks, work, and history? Moving from cultural programming and family conditioning to less ego identification, what of your identity will remain? What is your gold?

A midlife- and late-life crisis, understood in the framework of the Jungian psyche, is a time to confront one's shadows, those inner obstructions of development. A female may have issues with guilt from choosing a career over motherhood, self-doubt over her ability to be a good mother as she defines it, or shame from being molested as a child. Your shadows are all the causes for not manifesting an authentic life.

Working with an analyst during this period may take weeks or years, and the process ultimately ends with individuation where the client has recognized both her demons and her angels. Following the stages from confusion to chaos to confrontation, the final stage of purification, or insight, is the reunification of body and soul. Restructuring of the self with renewed focus and passion, usually in the guiding light of an archetype, is the foundation for a new life. One chooses to become a person living with a purpose. In this way, you deepen the experience of growing and claim your voice.

GRIEF RECOVERY

In her stages of grief, Dr. Elisabeth Kübler-Ross identifies the final stage as acceptance, which provides a platform for recovery for both the dying and loved ones. "Acceptance should not be mistaken for a happy stage. It is almost devoid of feelings," she writes. For the dying, acceptance is a time of letting go, of peace. For the family, ending the struggle with death is a time of recovery. The recovery process described by Dr. Kübler-Ross is also a process through which one can move through the "second maturity" and find meaning again. It is a stage of letting go, of detaching from the pain of loss, and beginning again.

Her definition of acceptance, though, is only the first step. If we allow ourselves to let go of being frozen in our loss, we will live more fully with the abilities we have available. We move from crisis to personal transformation. Finding the path of acceptance and love is possible. Renowned storyteller Michael Meade writes, "Our little encounters with death, sorrow, and loss are inevitable, and if suffered honestly can become the darker wisdom from which a greater life can grow. The territory of little-death is where the ego-self dies a little and a deeper revelation of life becomes more possible."

A little-death of the ego is the beginning of letting go of attachments. We may find the deeper revelation of life that Meade speaks of by seeing that our pain is connecting us to the pain of others, that we are not alone or unique but members of a cosmic story. We feel our interdependence with others, our world, our Earth. Grief recovery opens us to a new self and new sharing with others. We could not refer to our loss as "little encounters" if we didn't move on, away from the self-centered raw pain from which we began this journey.

In my case, I wouldn't call it crisis so much as desperation. I was writing a book and couldn't find my voice. My book, written with another author much younger than I, was about healing in nature. I had multiple sclerosis, and she had Lyme disease and we had a message to share, but my written words still came from a past that did not convey the personal. More than sixty years old, I still only had a stilted voice from academia and finance. How could I get real? By going into my pain. I'd hidden from feelings out of fear. What if I could not survive in this body? I had to let go of previous identities from school and career, which were reflected in my controlled and often contrived writing style. Academia and finance had been the core structures of my life success to that point. Writing a book to share my experience of disease and healing forced me to find myself as a storyteller. Stories are traditionally the bond of tribes, and for me, this was the beginning of a tribe as I created a friendship with a younger woman who sought to understand her experience of disease and healing. I found the self beneath the earlier identities and my writer's voice that could share my personal stories.

Grief is the doorway if we are brave enough. In our contemporary world, we have many excuses and distractions, addictions and debilitating depression, to hinder taking this journey, but divine grace is not limited. Alcoholics Anonymous participants begin by admitting they are powerless and turn their will and lives over to a Higher Power as they understand it. Later, in recovery, alcoholics turn the desperate need into a yearning for a deeper relationship with a Higher Power. As they take this step, grace holds their hands.

Letting go to seek a deeper love of the divine is the transformation the mystics sought and the new identity Jungians seek in alchemy. All are paths to initiation, the self, and an authentic inner being. Our disruptions and crises are gifts to guide us when we listen to the small voice within. Regardless of our years we still fear losing control. Maybe because of our years we fear losing control even more than before, yet letting go and trusting are essential to our growth now.

REFLECTIONS ON MY JOURNEY FROM OLDER TO ELDER

1. The inclination is to go backward to a safer place even though you know that time is past. Describe the ambivalence you are experiencing over giving up the life you have known and building a new life you don't yet know. You are taking a leap into the unknown.

2. Go deep inside. Go into the darkness and dare to inquire how you feel; ask for images to answer. It may be feelings of anger, abandonment, or confusion that come to you. Describe those images and feelings.

3. Then go further, deeper into your feelings. What appears or speaks to you? Describe what you have found. How did it begin? Where you are now? When you dare to face it, this disruption may almost overwhelm you.

4. What are you afraid of losing? Describe the ambivalence you are experiencing over giving up the life you have known and building a life you don't yet know.

5. What might be your new characteristics? How do they open you to a new beginning?

You are in the moment of potential transformation
if you are willing to press on.

Chapter Four

THE POWER OF INTUITION AND CREATIVITY

What is intuition? The English word intuition comes from the Latin *intueri*, which is translated as "to look inside" or "to contemplate." Intuition occupies a border state between thought and feeling and between the conscious and unconscious mind. Extrasensory ways of knowing, like intuition, are recognized as pathways to the morphic field of Jung's collective unconscious, as described by Dr. Jean Bolen in her book *Crossing to Avalon, A Woman's Midlife Quest for the Sacred*. The collective unconscious is where the most elemental beliefs shared by all human beings exist. When we act from this guidance, we are able to be with others in a deep way. We are given an understanding of their fears and passions, of their innermost desires, without their giving words to them.

Intuition refers to immediate apprehension by sense, a gut feeling, or an awareness of knowledge that is on the threshold of consciousness. It may come to us through our minds or our senses. It may be an inner direction to seek a new school for our child, or a different direction in our writing style from poetry to journal, or to choose another bench in the park. Some mystical traditions place the center of intuition in the third eye, which is the connection point to the soul. Human development theorists posit that females in older age develop wisdom that includes an enhanced capacity for intuition and interest in helping their communities. At this time in her life, a woman's intuitive power reaches beyond the previous focus on the immediate needs of self or family and becomes specifically attuned to supporting others.

Intuition is an important skill that allows us to recognize, judge, and predict people's intentions and situations. Interestingly, the concept of intuition and the unique understanding it brings is recognized in science and art across cultures and ages. Our intuition is a powerful mechanism for making decisions and shaping our experiences. True intuition is fragile, sensitive, and elusive; we may need to calm our usual hurried pace to experience it.

Because it is women who give birth, our instincts as women are tuned toward empathy, that special understanding of the needs of fellow beings, however small or large. This is referred to as empathic attunement. When intuition and empathy flow together, there is an intense affirmation of the self and, paradoxically, a transcendence of the self, a sense of the self as part of a larger whole. Another's well-being becomes as important as our own as our sense of separateness dissolves. According to researchers at the Stone Center of Wellesley College, this power of connection is an inherent ability we are given as females.

For tribal peoples, including Native Americans, empathic attunement is expressed through relationship with nature. They live in a universe where all beings, animate and inanimate, are interconnected. Nature is alive with divine forces. Shamans, the healers, travel beyond reality to alternate worlds to receive information. From these divine forces, they discover the cause of imbalances, whether in individuals, within the community, or between natural forces and the community. Knowing themselves to be a part of nature, tribal people don't have to overcome the belief of separation from their gods. Everything exists in balance, and every action requires care and respect for this delicate interdependence. To strive for balance in all matters is taught from childhood or intuitively grasped by tribal members and embodied by shamans.

Joy Harjo, poet laureate and a member of the Muscogee (Creek) Nation, tells a story of the connection native people have with the sacred and Mother Earth:

"There was a Navajo woman who lived far out on a reservation in a hogan, the traditional home of the indigenous people there. She was of a righteous nature, still prayed in the morning with cornmeal, took care of her sheep,

and was loved and well-respected by her neighbors. She was also blind. She was visited one day by the Holy Ones. As her hogan filled with the powerful presence of sacredness, the Holy Ones told her, as they towered over her, that they came to give a warning to the people.

"'We are nearing times where we will experience earth changes, famine, and strife, because people are forgetting their original teachings.' The Holy Ones instructed her to tell everyone to keep hold of their traditional ways, to remember prayer and to care for each other, for all things, for this Earth, or they will suffer."

-Joy Harjo

The living planet is our larger self. We are part of this system of living Earth. We belong to her. This profound sense can lead us to discover the voice of our intuition. Trusting the gift of intuition and the wisdom it reveals may come easily to a child, but in our mature years, we often doubt it. Life experiences and schooling have trained us to believe only what we can see and to act based on "rational" judgments. Thus, the pathway out of darkness may be hampered by our inability to trust the small inner voice speaking to us. Awakening our connection with nature and sense of belonging can help us find and open the door to our intuition. Contemporary women, like tribal peoples, may seek nature for spiritual grounding and encouragement. They may find daily practices of connecting to ocean waves, to birds in trees, or the trees themselves will support them on this journey.

As you listen and follow your intuitive guide, you may find that a new source of creative energy and inspiration flows into your life. Frances Vaughan, a transpersonal and humanistic psychologist in the seventies, examined the role of intuition in the creative process. She observed that a woman's intuition allows her to draw on "the infinite reservoir of the collective or universal unconsciousness, in which individual separateness and ego boundaries are transcended." These non-conscious mental states and the idea of supra-consciousness are important features in the creation of both visual art and music. They have the power to act as muses, inspiring our creativity.

When Pope John Paul II addressed artists on Easter Sunday in 1999, he wrote, "Overseeing the mysterious laws governing the universe, the divine breath of the Creator Spirit reaches out to human genius and stirs its creative power. He touches it with a kind of inner illumination which brings together the sense of the good and the beautiful, and he awakens energies of mind and heart which enable it to conceive an idea and give it form in a work of art."

In addition to providing inner illumination, as Pope John Paul suggested, the "voice within" or our intuition is a message from the divine that can stir our creativity. This powerful awareness, an unseen guide, allows us to view ourselves differently and to think in new, more creative ways. It can transform us.

If we choose to seek new meaning and purpose in our life, to take the pilgrim's path and enter the darkness, author Michael Meade affirms, "A true pilgrimage requires letting go of the very things most people try to hold onto. In seeking after what the soul desires we become pilgrims with no home but the path the soul would have us follow. As the old proverb says, 'Before you begin the journey, the journey owns you.'"

To get out of the darkness, we need to find the light of our souls. As Meade wrote, we become "pilgrims with no home" for a time, and then the "journey owns you." The journey owns us when we trust our intuition. We have taken a leap into the unknown, where we begin to cultivate our creative source, the gold of passion. Especially in our later years, when we feel ourselves following a deeper commitment and responding to the empathy we feel toward others, we are not alone. We may be working alone, but we no longer experience ourselves as separate. We feel even more alive when we are given a new passion, or new depth of commitment.

I once read a dissertation on inspiration in which a woman reported her experience of crisis in a country that erupted in violence. After months of feeling immobilized in her home and afraid to go out, she felt her own "crack in an armor of predictability to a transformational, inspirational experience" of becoming an artist. She later described awakening to a light trance, a flow state, and experiencing a wave of inspiration. She reported discovering herself as a creator and learning that creativity is a value above previous achievements and goals and that wonderful images and beauty held as much meaning for her as prior academic, income-generating world views. The possibility of creative responses to our inner voice is a gift in the later years. We may embrace a muse's call to creativity or respond to an invitation to care for the forest or our fellow beings. The essence is that we create, and in this way, contribute to improving the world and the lives of others.

Most of us who have taken this "pilgrimage" would never have imagined ourselves on the path we now walk or even capable of what we are doing at this late stage in life.

For Dr. Gene Cohen, who founded the National Center on Aging, "there is no denying the problems that accompany aging. But what has been universally denied is the potential. The ultimate expression of potential is creativity." Winston Churchill, who had never before lifted a paintbrush, took to oil painting in his retirement after winning the war and a Nobel Prize. His dedication led him to produce more than five hundred paintings and to write a book, *Painting as a Pastime,* on a subject that had rarely held his attention in his earlier life pursuits. Dr. Cohen's research has shown an amazing connection between creativity and brain health. Creativity in later life is more than a release from previous societal restrictions but may reflect biological changes. In fact, creativity and intuition may be related in the brain, as both seem to be revealed beneath the surface of ordinary consciousness.

As you illuminate and develop the energy and passion within, you may realize you have found your inner calling, which was invisible for much of your life. Now, as Dr. James Hollis, a Jungian psychologist, explains, you discover that "we all have a calling. For some it will be found in our capacity for caring for the needs of the suffering world around us. For others it will be the work of hands. For some it will be the work of the mind that opens doors and shatters shackles. For still others it will be the exploration of the natural world. For some it will be pushing back the boundaries of our limited sense of the possible. But for all us, there is a large summons."

We can turn to our inner direction where intuition, empathic attunement, creativity, and play will show us the way. Whether we choose psychoanalysis, a Christian or Native American path, or Kabbalah in Judaism, the doorway is the same. On the threshold of consciousness, our guide awaits us. We have a sharpened ability to access our intuition in our later years as females if we open to it with trust.

REFLECTIONS ON MY JOURNEY
FROM OLDER TO ELDER

1. What light within (perhaps a flicker, maybe a bolt of lightning) has moved you out of your stuck place? Is there a sense of something calling you from this place of inspiration? What is it saying to you? Dialogue with the inner voice, seek what meaning and new awareness may be within.

2. How can you be more curious about this bit of inspiration? Does it refer to a myth? Write about it. Talk with a trusted friend about it. Work with the flicker that is a light in your chaos.

3. On your journey, you will have a small voice to guide you. Does it suggest some direction for you to move? Is it pointing you to experiment in some way in your life that is new and waiting for you to pursue? What might that be?

4. Let your creativity and intuition take over. Can you recall a dream or inner desire you didn't attend to earlier in your life? What were the obstacles or challenges that got in your way?

5. In our early lives, we had to follow a path, to attend school, get good grades, and then find a job and a husband. Now we do not have the expectations of others to influence our personal choices. In later life the individual is not expected to perform, either to fill the roles of career or parent of earlier years. Imagine what you may become.

Experience this new freedom.
Let your intuition and creativity take you.

Chapter Five

MONIKA

Although Monika is not an elder, at least not in years, the story of her crisis and transformation speaks to the process of self-discovery that can awaken us to our gifts in our later years. Monika readily acknowledges that her recovery from a terminal diagnosis was the beginning of her life as a depth psychologist and astrologer. She was in her late twenties when the medical world predicted she would die in several weeks. She had stage 4 ovarian cancer, and there were no remaining arrows in the quiver to kill it. Her dreams, Monika believes, cured her by leading the healing energies to fight their battle successfully to a "miraculous recovery."

Her recovery was an initiation, an opening to the life of a healer, and to helping others discover their self-healing abilities. In her own words: "one ought to be close to death to have the freedom to talk about it… it's not a shining badge, it's actually been an arduous part of my life experience. I have been close to death a number of times and on the borderline a number of times in my life." After the prognosis of two weeks to live, Monika was at the mercy of her psyche, and she courageously uncovered the will and inner wisdom to move beyond the reality she knew. She was not directed by the healing powers of others to fix her but discovered her own source for healing from the inside, as close to the bone as it gets.

She recounted a dream she had during a Shrink Wrap Radio interview with Dr. Dave. The dream helped her discover the amazing amount of intelligence that lives in our psyche and can come to assist us.

"Basically, a part of the dream included a doctor with whom I was speaking, and he said, 'listen, I'm sorry, I know you just came to draw blood, but I actually have to do a hysterectomy.'

"In the dream, I was incredibly upset by this and replied, 'What are you talking about? How can this be?'

"And then he said, 'Don't take it personally because there really are two wombs, and you still have the other one.'

"And then I could see that there was this womb made of some kind of subtle essence which I still would have after the hysterectomy. Well, I had no idea that I had ovarian cancer when I had this dream. As synchronicity happens,

I was going in for a regular checkup after this, and the doctor immediately said, 'you have to go in for exploratory surgery. Something's wrong.'

"And I immediately flashed on the dream. It let me know something from the psyche could see me before I could see myself. And also that it could speak to me, it could imagine it, and of course I knew then that that's where I would be turning to find a way to make it through that process, a step at a time, reaching out for help from the dream world that could see the process I was engaged in."

When we cry out in a time of need, Monika is convinced the psyche gets a chance—the ego consciousness gets a chance—to reach beyond the domination of rationality. "We're starved for the mythopoetic imagination in our world. The rationalistic… culture of science has buried the imaginal," Monika said when we sat down for an interview. "A reservoir of the unconscious is alive and well in the depths of the human psyche, of the human soul. And it is infinitely capable of regenerating itself and coming up inside our own human experience… You know, something's always on the throne of consciousness in our culture. We've had rationalism there forever which kills off anything to do with the imagination, the imaginal. What is going on underneath each psyche, as it was going on underneath mine, is this reservoir of the unconscious. It is alive, a well in the depths of the human psyche, of the human soul. It is infinitely capable of regenerating itself and coming up inside our own human experiences."

Monika's healing and the life she gained after her crisis are a remarkable testimony to the power of the Chiron allegory, not as a myth but as a story of initiation and healing. In Monika's case, her whole life had fallen apart: her body, her marriage, her academic program. Then her dreams revealed the underworld. During this experience, a healing presence took her hand. Being guided by the dream spirit, she found the energy of rebirth. For many in our chaotic world who suffer from physical and psychic pain, it is Chiron, the ancient hero of Greek mythology and wounded healer archetype, who opens the door to another dimension. Chiron, the icy body orbiting the sun, was discovered in the sky in 1977 and since has become a new astrological presence. Originally classified as an asteroid, now identified as a new class of centaurs that is both a minor planet and comet, its influence as an archetypal entity continues to expand. We will now explore the Chiron myth of the wounded healer with Monika's words.

"Chiron's wound in Greek mythology comes when he, as the leader of the centaurs, trots out of his cave responding to a commotion happening among the rowdier centaurs. A stray arrow from Hercules' bow lands in Chiron's thigh (sometimes seen as his foot) and no one can help him get it out or heal it, neither the deities nor the great shamans. So, he crawls off to his cave alone to connect with the invisible realms in search of healing.

"In some versions of the myth, the poison in the arrow is impossible to heal and Chiron finds that the transformation required is to become human,

accept this fate, and die. In terrible pain, he prays to the gods to allow him to die and they, in gratitude for his teachings, grant him mortality, which is a deep gift of mercy. After his death, the gods grant him radiant life in the night sky as one of the eternal ones. He trades his immortality for mortality (exchanging fates with Prometheus who then is no longer being punished for bringing fire to human beings), and Chiron experiences mortality as grace and eventually becomes a constellation in the sky.

"The dictum healer, heal thyself and thus the world belongs to the archetypal pattern of Chiron and to all of us who are touched by it. Through this pattern, one's healing is the medicine, becomes part of the medicine, that flows through the person and into the world in the form of the sharing of the flow of new consciousness, healing modalities, creative awakening, love, insight and more."

By exploring the pain within, we become like Chiron, humbling ourselves and giving up the illusion of control to become healers of ourselves and others. By entering another world, that of the psyche, the imaginal is infinitely capable of creating new life. Monika guides others into their imaginations to work with their psyches. They become rebirthed through connection with images and experiences of the inner world. Like the wounded healer Chiron, we become our own healers. In Monika's view, our woundedness is the doorway to our awakening, and into a greater fullness or wholeness and also more in the truth of who we are. Through trauma, we find ourselves.

As teacher and guide, she frequently lectures on Carl Jung and leads trips abroad. Immersion in different cultures gives her the chance to feel different archetypal energies; in Cuba or Ireland, unique stories and songs emerge. Steeped in mythology, Ireland is a magical setting where nymphs and elves peek from each rock and visitors drink from the living waters of Irishman William Yeats's poetry. The imaginal world is alive with energy. Although a visit may be short in duration, the depth of memories and potential of awakening archetypes previously unfelt make a two-week visit the journey of a lifetime. Waking up to the beauty of myth and culture in another country infuses us with that energy.

In Monika's life, even before her initiation and transformation of unexplained recovery, she was devoted to pursuing her calling. From a college student studying mice in a laboratory, she became an impassioned student of Jung. By absolute need, she followed her dreams as they unfolded, and she went to Switzerland for a nine-year program of study at the von Franz-Jungian Institute. After decades working as a Jungian analyst, unlocking the dream world of others, and writing her voluminous work *Pregnant with Darkness, Alchemy and the Rebirth of Consciousness*, Monika continues her life in nature.

Enjoying beaches and coyotes, Monika is a part-time resident of a ranch in California and oversees her healing center in Tesuque, New Mexico. Under the spacious sky in the land of enchantment, she brings her clients closer to their dreams, to the wisdom within, to make sense of their lives. Somewhere in our lives, we receive invitations for healing, and then everything else comes out of that. We work with our own wounds, and we work on our own healing, and then we have the capacity to be reborn. Monika demonstrates the possibility of a new life, of rebirth following trauma. Her academic background in clinical psychology and her work with the von Franz Institute were a mere beginning to her lifelong learning from the dreams of others that followed.

Monika impresses on women the importance of joining with other women in their healing journeys and getting back to the land. Who will be present with us while we go through a deep journey is extremely important. As explorers together, women find meaning for their lives and discover their unique healing gifts. Having the companionship of women and not being afraid to ask for help, including help from other realms, are essential. Harmony with others and with nature gives us the footing to reach into our imaginations. As we allow our perceptions to change in nature, our paradigms shift. It is a reprieve for the nervous system as our minds are calmed. No longer are we handcuffed by patriarchy but experience a light within. In Monika's words, "a lightbulb morning replaces the darkness;" the conceptual mind dims, and we are inside the body of nature. Returning to the poetic world of Yeats:

> *O chestnut tree, great rooted blossomer,*
> *Are you the leaf, the blossom or the bole?*
> *O body swayed to music, O brightening glance,*
> *How can we know the dancer from the dance?*
>
> (William Butler Yeats, "Among School Children")

Where realms of consciousness intertwine, nature is the vessel that holds us. Monika draws from her personal medical recovery and her closeness to nature as aides to find the connection to deal with the physical or psychic woundedness in others. She upholds that anyone who goes through the darkness can find the dream spirit guides and energy. The dream spirit, she believes, is the spirit of nature itself. "Hopefully," she says, "through the healing, something grows, something living happens out of it and may also energize the world with the capacity to heal. The healing modalities may lead to a new perspective or new vision. The healing modalities open us to fuller consciousness to help heal." Dreams are a pathway to healing from within. They will show a person the previously unrecognized value of who they are. The collective world soul is strong, and Monika proposes this healing is happening around the globe.

Monika has also studied the art of astrology. She is fascinated by the ever-changing world above. Since the discovery of Chiron, the tales of the stars have expanded to include the energies of the healer, whose powers are blocked or empowered by various alignments. In an era of ecological sickness, the Chiron archetype and energy above may guide us. Compassion and empathy, considered to be gifts of Chiron in mythology, are entering our consciousness even when wars erupt and greed encompasses our planet.

The discovery of Chiron in the sky was the beginning of waves of awakening. A new paradigm is arising. As we become more instinctual and develop greater compassion, we become more unified. Other cultures, such as the Irish, may be closer already to the shift. The Celtic mythology and their closeness to the land with the psyche of place impress visitors with lifelong memories. Monika's groups have indelible imprints of a new-to-them sacredness of people and place. Leprechauns and fairies and nature elves share their worlds. There's a definite "soul change that brings inspiration from the Irish people… a drop in the bucket of world awakening."

Monika continues to lecture internationally on mythology and symbolism, dreams and wellness, alchemy and creativity while taking several trips a year internationally to lead students in deep inner explorations. She has helped many with her understanding of the writings of Jung, his dreams and her own, and the world of mythology. Her fascination with the unconscious and desire to guide others in this exploration has only grown over the decades. I hope these pages provide a sense of the beauty of her empathic ability and teachings. As a Chiron figure, she remains among us to continue healing and inspiring us to become fuller, more open dreamers. Monika embodies the spirit of an elder.

Reflections on My Journey
from Older to Elder

1. Does this woman's life story resonate with you? In what ways?

2. Monika's medical challenges and healing crisis are unique to her, but you may have a similar episode in your life, whether life-threatening or critical to your existence in some way. Monika sought her dreams for inner guidance and found an archetype to guide her. Describe a dream that may have given you encouragement or a different perspective on the crisis.

3. Recall a situation that brought a guiding presence or sudden awareness that was healing or simply showed you a new possibility.

4. Monika looks to Chiron as her archetype of the wounded healer. Can you also find resonance with this archetype? In what ways? If you were wounded emotionally as a child or in your later years hurt physically, you may now have a desire to save others from similar harm.

Chapter Six

LYNDA

While her parents pursued their careers studying to become Jungian analysts, they sent Lynda to her grandparents' ranch in California. She arrived from London as a child, dressed in a frock from the city, and didn't feel like she belonged in such an environment. She rolled up in a car from the thirties, with running boards and strange headlamps, a vehicle rarely seen on the ranch where horses were the familiar mode of transport. Ranch children were fascinated by her arrival, clinging to the vehicle and frightening Lynda. To her, they seemed "like monkeys, covered with dirt, presenting big smiles and strange expressions of joy." Just seven years old, she had a new world ahead of her.

Supervising children was not a priority on the 39,000-acre Hollister ranch. Lynda and her brother, both newcomers from England, were the fourth generation but didn't gain special attention over the cattle, horses, and chickens. "The feeling of having to figure out everything for myself, with no help from people or nature, was pervasive. And so it was for everyone. We had to go it alone." First thing in the morning, the children were whisked out of the house and disappeared up into the canyons or down to the beach. Lynda recalls that it was lonely and scary, but she learned to accept and eventually relish the solitude. Even as a very young child in England, it was a dog, Judy, "a smallish, furry beast," who had sustained her as an intimate buddy. She was unprepared for the unfamiliar world of California ranching, where battling among the other children, hoping to gain approval if not affection, would fill the next five years. It was clearly a culture shock.

Even for the youngest, ranch life involved tough matters like participating in castrating calves and witnessing the often raw and violent struggle to survive. Lynda vividly remembers a frog's head and front legs (arms!) still visible as it croaked and clawed while being devoured by a snake. Such moments formed her, teaching her that life in the wilderness is not for the faint of heart; ruthlessness marked the survivor. She learned to fall off a pony and get back on, aware that the other children had given her the most difficult mount. Within a year, she was on her own exploring the beaches and streambeds, trusting the four legs beneath her, knowing that somehow even the steepest, narrowest paths wouldn't daunt the oldest of ponies as she waited her turn to get on a cow horse. Then she would ride with the cowboys, steering calves when they veered from the group, running to catch up with the runaways.

It may have been the experience of riding, first a pony then a fuller-sized horse, that taught Lynda how to meld with nature; carried by the movement of a horse and depending on that other being, traveling together across the windswept beaches, two bodies in a dance together as one. Trusting the other to know where to place those four feet to climb a steep trail allows the rider to surrender control. A child connects with nature without questioning and learns self-protection by acquiring courage and stamina. Growing up on the land was a gift to Lynda, nurturing her imagination to dream with the birds and butterflies. Although she was not close to the other youngsters, she acquired toughness and self-reliance. Her childhood was forever about struggle and finding self-confidence, about learning to take care of herself in nature and finding support and solace in the wilderness, merging with her horse and nature by the sea.

After marrying and having children, Lynda wanted her path to be different from her mother's, so she chose to make family, not a career, her priority; however, having been abandoned by her mother when she was little, Lynda only knew how to be a mother in defiance. She could provide shelter and food but lacked the joy of motherhood. Finally deciding to pursue academic training, her mothering years did not exactly end, but she fell back on her years as a child on the ranch, trusting that her children's instincts would protect them. Lynda allowed her teenagers to explore the "wilderness" of San Francisco while she returned to class. Allowing her children to discover for themselves the meaning of flower children, to explore on their own, was their education while she pursued hers. It was a wilderness, wild and unexplored, revealing new ways of being, teaching them to rely on themselves.

Jungian analysts were popular and younger than Lynda. She was thirty-seven when she began her career. In addition to her age, she struggled to establish close affiliations with her clients until she was confronted by three hippie-type clients who told her to loosen up and "get real." They objected to her distant style and challenged her to open up and share her feelings. The student culture of the time was keen to explore both drugs and self, to push all boundaries, rebelling against most authority.

Lynda's life on the ranch had taught her more about fitting in, not questioning those above her. She had a lot to learn beyond the books to become a therapist. As she grappled with her new career and the complications of getting licensed as a psychotherapist, she doubted the meaning of life. A brief affair with a professor was merely a symptom of her searching for something more, seeking an escape from the dark place those years were for her.

Facing their common challenge of marriage and aging, Lynda and her husband Klaus decided to climb a mountain that they had only seen from the air on a trip to Russia. Trekking the Hindu Kush was a questionable choice. She and Klaus, with minimal miles charted or experience hiking with a backpack, undertook the Himalayas in Pakistan, a country just opening its borders to travelers. Not having had trekkers from abroad for many years, Pakistan lacked the infrastructure for hikers. Even porters and maps were limited. Lynda and her husband joined a few intrepid strangers to climb the peaks with a guide who had never been on the trail.

Unfortunately, Klaus's backpack was lost in transit, and he was without hiking boots, only loafers for the weeks ahead and the 15,000-foot elevation passes to climb. Lynda writes in her book *Time Out of Mind* that after leaving a town with a bazaar where everything was dirty or broken, and only fly-covered tea to drink, it was her inner power of endurance from a childhood on the ranch that enabled her to continue for miles and miles on the rocky trails. Cliff roads that provided entry on sheer rock faces were an almost pleasant memory compared to the endless foggy cold mornings and sweltering heat of goat trails that followed. Unbearable heat was replaced by unpredictable avalanches in steep passes.

Lynda and Klaus now split away from the others, choosing to leave an inexperienced leader who was determined, without sufficient resources or even a map, to cross yet more mountainous passes. They proceeded in a geography so foreign and hostile they were unable to be awed by the mystical mountains beyond. "We had little to say, or think; we were just there, immersed in heat and the sound of thunder." They pushed themselves beyond their physical limits for another trudge up steep switchbacks where Lynda kept telling herself, "One foot, the other foot: the sun was fierce on my head, even through the umbrella shield. I became disembodied again. I felt nothing under my boots; the strain in my legs and the pain in my shoulders from the pack didn't belong to me. I floated inside myself, without thought or consciousness, suspended in space. Everything went still, and I was no longer a person—just a sense of continuity, a spot flowing along."

This arduous journey brought a new awareness to Lynda that changed her approach to being a psychoanalyst. She recognized for the first time how central intimacy is to the process of working with a client in therapy. "When I finally understood that this intimacy was similar to the connection I felt with the wilderness, I realized what it was that made psychology so natural a field of work for me." Lynda was grounded again by the sense of bonding she had felt with the horses on the ranch and of being immersed within the vast coastal wilderness where she was raised. As a therapist, she "realized that I needed not to do anything. Best was if I sat with people as witness and took in their experience as much as possible. Make space for them. Care about them. Be with them." Like her work as a therapist, melding with nature required a willingness to move in unison without controlling or knowing what would unfold. On returning months later from Pakistan, she realized she had departed during a mid-life crisis when she had been ambivalent to her life. Lynda found a new commitment and vowed deeply to accept the gift of her life, to follow her career as therapist with her husband in the wild land of Maine. Both could continue their careers in the grace of wilderness.

Reflections on My Journey from Older to Elder

1. Did you learn something about yourself in reading Lynda's story? Do you recall a memory from your childhood where you felt joined to nature? Perhaps a family dog or tree in the backyard gave comfort or a sense of something bigger than yourself. Write down your thoughts.

2. What strength or inner sense of belonging did you receive?

3. Does Lynda's story of struggle with authority figures in her professional life resonate? How so?

4. Have you wanted to break away, or have you, in some small or large way, challenged yourself to try and change a demanding situation? What did you learn from it?

5. If you are a parent, can you identify experiences from your childhood you were able or wished to recreate for your children? Are you feeling held back from making changes in your life because you worry it will impact your children? Perhaps your children are grown, and you want to give them guidance. What would you like to tell them? Being a parent is an incredible role, and sometimes we need to take a step back to remember what other parts of ourselves we still wish to develop and explore.

Chapter Seven

SUSAN

Susan's fascination with music began at a very young age before she was even in kindergarten. "I had an affinity for it," she remembers with a smile, for the choir singing in church, for the music played on the radio in her home. Once in school, she began learning to play herself. The classroom instruments were the source of her joy, and when they came to recruit kids for the school band, she met the band director, who gave her a flute. Although her mother told Susan she wouldn't be good enough to be a performer, the other option for a female in music in the sixties was teaching. Being a determined young girl, Susan knew she didn't want to be like other teachers who she thought ordinary.

Susan was drawn to a level of music not often considered appropriate for the young. She had an appreciation of their internal, emotional responses, how the music made them feel. She was not interested in policing a band of youngsters hammering away on whatever instruments they were handed from the music closet. In the beginning of her career as a music teacher, Susan decided she would become a very unconventional one. She didn't believe music to be simply a matter of learning the notes; it was also about listening. She was launching into a whole new discipline of study. She sought to awaken sensitivities to music in her young students.

Listening with passion is not a common approach to music education, even for most music appreciation classes. Susan was intrigued by the effect of music on herself, how it made her laugh and cry and experience a sense of awe. Her ability to close her eyes and imagine was something unique. She could listen and become permeated by the music; it wasn't just her ears that received it, but her whole body. The schools where she worked continued asking her to teach in a traditional elementary-school manner, while the universities still weren't giving her the interdisciplinary approach she sought, even at the master of education level. Susan knew what she wanted to study and write about, what courses she wanted to follow, but academia wasn't ready for her.

She decided to create a research project about her students, beginning with fourth graders and their emotional responses to music. The university she was attending showed an interest in her project about exploring how music is "processed." She described it as an aesthetic experience that would take a dictionary to describe, but her emphasis would be on listening. She finished her master degree and moved to Ohio to teach in a public school and, more importantly, to attend lectures of the professor who would become her mentor. The way he talked about the concepts of art and music, in terms of color and shape, resonated with her. These were the very ideas she had been seeking. Again, for Susan, music was much more than the notes that composed it.

The philosophy of this one man inspired her to drop her teaching position to pursue a doctoral degree. Susan's ideas would have been Jungian in the late twentieth century, but she didn't even know of Carl Jung then, nor did most others in middle-America educational institutions. In a graduate program, it's the university that is supposed to shape the student. Susan had a very strong sense of the direction she wanted to pursue, and when it didn't fit the existing program in a school, she found another. Even today, she insists she always "cut her own groove."

This period in Susan's life was a turning point. She identified not only her interests but a school where she could pursue them. The key to her turning was a series of losses, beginning with the sudden passing of her doctoral advisor. Susan asked the officiants if she could bring some music to the memorial service for this woman with whom she had so quickly become deeply bonded. Susan was familiar with a variety of songs and had a guitar and could sing. It was something she did in church. Prior to entering the university, a close member of the choir had passed, and, without questioning, Susan joined others in playing music at her memorial. This was unconventional at the time. Because of this experience, she was allowed to play for her advisor. In Susan's words, "It was a glorious thing, because we're all so close to this woman and we were there to be able to sing her out."

That same year Susan's father also died. She was able to make a weekend trip to visit him at his bedside and brought her guitar. It was with him that she first experienced the gift of sharing music with a loved one who was dying, and she sang him to sleep before he passed. This opportunity showed her that she could give to others departing this life in this special way. Music gets inside, even for a patient who is comatose, who no longer has access to verbal language. Susan believed she could share solace and love with her voice and guitar and music as the universal language. She vowed that if she could find a way to be with people with music and allow music to be the communication, that would be her ideal job. There was no such avenue at that time. Hospice music therapy did not exist yet.

Growing up, Susan's father had always told her not to worry where the money will come from; if she wanted to do something badly enough and felt there was strong merit in it, just do it. So she finished her doctorate in less than three years. She quickly landed a position as an assistant professor at the University of Maine in the music department, packed her things, and drove off to begin teaching. As before in Susan's life, her independence and insight allowed her to soon become the outlier in her department. As peers worried about getting a child into choir or the marching band, Susan's thoughts were on the child, fourth grader or first grader, and how they experienced music. As a teacher of elementary students, she was not concerned with their performance or with pushing them into a successful music career. In her years of teaching students of all ages, only two went on to become professional performers. Susan's deepest interest, though, was to become involved with what was now emerging as hospice, to use her music with patients. As she was researching the possibilities in Maine and getting involved with a hospice team, she attended a conference with a booth about music and guided imagery. This was her introduction to the Bonny Method and Carl Jung.

Helen Bonny was an amazing violinist from a musical family who started her training at the age of five. When Helen first heard a violin, she became enamored that only four strings could make such music. She studied the instrument through college. In a journal for music therapy, Helen is quoted: "Of inestimable value was the training of the ear to discern pitch variations, to detect tonal color, to translate feeling responses into musical dynamics..." From playing the violin, rehearsing, performing, working in ensembles and orchestras, she described how she "uncovered abilities of concentration, communication, and timing that would become assets in attaining academic achievement and later, in enhancing social ease and business acumen...It was during my study of violin at Oberlin with Reber Johnson...that I learned through hours of practice and careful instruction that producing the correct tone is not enough. The skill of the performer and the intention behind their playing are the two elements required to make music."

Years later, in 1948, a life-changing moment occurred while Helen was rehearsing with her accompanist. "It was as if the violin was not my own; bow arm and fingers were held in abeyance/obedience to a light and wonderful infusion that created an unbelievable sound I knew I had not ever produced before. The notes mellowed and soared with exquisite grace. The tones soared with an ease and purity beyond the boundaries of remembered sound." After that epiphany, Helen believed the magic that had happened for her could happen for others, that there might be a way to enter and uncover the creative potential in each person through carefully chosen music.

She went on to develop her method and discover compositions suited for her program. Later, she became Director of the Music Therapy Program at Catholic University, performed music research at the Maryland Psychiatric Research Center, completed her PhD at Union Graduate School, and founded the Institute for Consciousness and Music to provide training in the method she was developing in the seventies. It came to be known as the Bonny Method of Guided Imagery and Music (GIM). As an exploration of depth psychotherapy, the method is a way to access and work with the creative unconscious, utilizing music to deeply relax and allow the client to enter an altered state. The therapist's role is to support the client in engaging with sounds and images as they unfold during a session.

The healing power of music to guide us to the wisdom of the psyche, with or without psychedelics, is a key to both the Bonny Method and Susan's intuitive work with hospice patients. The same passionate inquiry that motivated Helen Bonny also motivated Susan. Helen's work became Susan's inspiration from that first introduction. Learning of another's curiosity about music, of how a performer might "get inside the music" so that it speaks to the listener's spirit and sensitivity, was tremendously powerful and validating.

Touching buried emotions or forgotten memories is the magic of music. Although the two only met once, Susan remarked that Helen was a quiet, lovely person. Both were musicians and explorers of the spirit seeking the healing power of music as a guide.

They knew their music opened another realm and could assist in exploring consciousness and healing. Music therapy was a new modality of depth psychology and was just being developed. In the sixties, Helen came to the attention of researchers in plant-based psychedelics. They wanted to understand how to use psychedelics with patients and were curious about the possibilities of using music to enhance the therapeutic process. They asked Helen to participate, and she provided the guided imagery. During her early work with hospice, Susan didn't act as a therapist but utilized Helen's theory and her own intuition to select musical pieces. Gauging a client's or subject's mood is key to the effectiveness of musical pieces in guiding them through the layers of consciousness.

On one occasion, Susan entered a hospital room to find an older woman sitting beside her comatose husband. The wife asked Susan if she knew the song "Danny Boy." She did and began to play and softly sing. The wife then began to talk about the trips they had taken as a couple, recalling memories, asking her husband if he remembered when they were in Ireland. Though the doctors had considered him unconscious, he could still hear. The entire body is the organ for listening. As Susan often says, "You don't need your brain on board to hear." The following week Susan returned to the hospital to ask how the husband was doing. His medical team had not expected him to live very long, and Susan was shocked to learn that the day after she had been there, he had walked out of the hospital with his wife. That's one extraordinary tale of the power of music.

Another true story involved a huge family who had gathered around a patient's bed. The patient was already in a coma. After Susan entered the hospital room and introduced herself, the granddaughter turned to the older woman next to her and said, "Mama, this lady plays music." The woman kind of looked at her, and then the younger lady looked back at Susan and said, "Yes, please play." Susan asked if "Amazing Grace" would be all right, and the woman nodded. "I started that song," Susan recalls, "and it was (like) a domino effect around the room. People started with tears. All the way around the room. And by the time I was done there was such a different feel to the space." The elder woman put her arms around Susan, not letting her depart and ignoring the huge guitar hanging between them. Amid the hug, she said thank you. The family needed that experience of soothing and release; the music was something familiar to all. It brought them together as a family in grief, and they departed together in spirit.

Susan worked with hospice for over twenty years. During the COVID pandemic, it was no longer possible to enter patients' rooms, and Susan moved away to join her family in Maine where she continued to offer therapy sessions to her psychotherapy clients via video. Her passion and curiosity for music have not waned; in fact, the week before our interview, she said she had attended an online conference about music and the use of ketamine (ecstasy chemical) as a healing modality. The growing interest in using currently illegal substances for healing has renewed actions to bring street-named acid and ecstasy back for medicinal use. Hearing academics discuss the use of music with ketamine-assisted therapy, Susan knew she could do a better job at using music to guide individuals to a deeper level of themselves. Her whole life has been working in this world, in books and with patients, in music and with verbal language, and after all her training, she could do a better job!

Maybe her twenty years of experience are giving her a mandate to continue, calmly listening to her dad's words, "If it's meant to be, don't worry where the money will come from." But in her elder years, the issue is not money; it's a lack of energy. More centers may arise for research into music and drugs, but perhaps the path now is for younger folks. Whether Susan will embark on another stage in her career remains to be seen. Her inspiration from Helen Bonny to pursue decades of work with hospice has touched the hearts and souls of many patients and their families in moments where few others could.

For now, Susan encourages all of us to simply take the time to listen and use music as therapy. We must come with compassionate inquiry when working with ourselves as well as others. Allow a quiet moment first to honor the silence. Then with eyes closed, play a selected piece of music. Just listen. It doesn't matter if it's familiar or unfamiliar. Listen. When the music is finished, when that magic is done, spend some more quiet time. Even without psychedelics, we can experience altered states and feel closer to spirit, using music as therapy. That is the fundamental premise of Bonny's and Susan's work.

Reflections on My Journey
from Older to Elder

1. What would you like to ask of Susan if you could meet her? Does her story of seeking a more well-matched-for-her course of study or work practice resonate?

2. What aspects of her crisis, the death of so many close to her in a short period, seem similar to your dark place?

3. What ability or passion in your life may be similar to Susan's for music? You may have developed a yearning to travel or garden or study history that has become a gift for you to share with others. What might this be?

4. Perhaps your special ability is not yet accepted as a gift. Susan's ability to play a musical instrument wasn't notable until she joined it with caring for folks in hospice. Where do you imagine your gift may hide?

Chapter Eight

RACHEL

Santa Barbara is a lovely town in Southern California, a tourist destination that attracts visitors from around the world. Those who visit, though, rarely encounter the homeless men and women who walk the streets at night or early morning and otherwise seem to slip out of view. For many of us who reside here, the homeless exist beneath the radar because we have turned away. We don't see them. We blame them for starting fires at their encampments or being bothersome and unpleasant in front of stores and restaurants, but still, we don't see them. Rachel, however, has been finding ways to care for those living on the streets since her first visit to Santa Barbara in 2003.

As a woman from the Midwest, and a female controller in the male-dominated bastion of Ford Motor Company, Rachel couldn't stand the thought of someone going hungry when she was well-fed. She saw the ragged forms huddled in corners on State Street as human beings, not just nuisances. Each time she visited, she and her husband looked for the individuals they had seen before, eager to extend a helping hand. Upon retiring, they moved to this charming enclave, and Rachel became passionately dedicated to her outreach effort.

Raised in a Dutch community on a dairy farm, she was the seventh of nine children. She was brought up Dutch Reformed, an extremely strict and judgmental denomination. No drinking, dancing, bowling, smoking, or movies were allowed. Everything was forbidden except going to church, and twice on Sunday. Today, the Dutch Reformed Church is regarded as evangelical. When she moved away, she began to let go, unlearning the strict indoctrination of her youth. This was a liberating process of self-discovery for Rachel. Through traveling, more than thirty trips to South America and Europe, and participating in numerous spiritual programs, she has sought to expand her worldview and learn about other cultures, religions, and ways of life. Working with and befriending the homeless has taught her about their anxieties and phobias and helped her gain a deeper understanding of her struggles. Often the most difficult challenge is continuing when the women she desperately wants to help reject her care.

Relinquishing religious rules did not require turning away from her family. Rachel attributes her mother's generosity with instilling in her a desire to take care of others.

She describes her mother as an angel who "was so kind, sweet and respectful of everyone. She never went anywhere without bringing a gallon of milk, a dozen eggs, a fresh loaf of bread, or some of her crocheted items. I think this is where I got my desire to feed people." The role model her mother presented guides Rachel's altruism today, deepened by the teachings of Father Richard Rohr and his open disagreement with many of the Catholic church's policies. Her everyday passion closely follows his message to shed ego to gain greater closeness to spirit.

It takes a long time to develop a relationship of trust with a person living on the streets because of mental illness. Their personal history often makes them suspicious and afraid. The book *Street Crazy* by Stephen Seager helped shape and inform Rachel's understanding of the mentally ill. Dr. Seager traces the problem of mental illness and ostracized individuals in the community as far back in history as the Greeks and Arabs of 30 AD. The cause of mental illness, whether it be demons or chemistry, has been debated over the millennia since, and methods of care have likewise changed. In ancient times, the Egyptians built asylums designed to care for the mentally ill and offered recreational therapy, including boat trips on the Nile and music, teaching them to create and enjoy.

In contrast, mentally ill street people in America in the twenty-first century are caught in a legal system that returns them to the streets after seventy-two hours of care in a hospital. Decades of "deinstitutionalization" have taken away a coordinated support system. Overstretched by the needs of drug addicts and suicidal victims, neighborhood clinics don't have the resources or training, and supervision of prescribed medicines is non-existent. The volunteer work of individuals like Rachel is a gift, an attempt to continue the ancient ethic of treating the mentally ill with dignity.

In the beginning, a woman named Christine, who only much later gave her name, would refuse the sandwich Rachel offered. Rachel thought she must be deaf or mute but kept searching for her to see what she needed. Christine's childhood memory of seeing her sick mother in a hospital before she passed was terrifying. Then her grandmother took her in, but she also died. This loss left young Christine with an alcoholic father who rented rooms in the home to other alcoholic men. Though she never shared it, Rachel assumes these men abused Christine. As a street person, Christine never allowed herself to lie down, recognizing her vulnerability as a woman. She slept sitting against the wall of a restaurant or outside the art museum. Her location changed often because she had been run out of "her places" when authorities dealt with complaints against the homeless. One night, a homeless man with a bottle of alcohol came into her alcove. Christine screamed, and another homeless man came to rescue her. Rachel has learned that there is community, even for those on the streets.

When Rachel speaks of the beginning of her outreach, she recalls, "I was obsessed with the homeless, especially Christine. It took years for me to create balance in my life. I thought about them the first thing in the morning, during the day when I encountered them, and at night before dozing off. If I woke up in the middle of the night, I thought about them." Rachel wanted to help and make the homeless comfortable, and she admits that maybe she was trying to fix them. She offered to take Christine to social services and would watch her grocery cart so she could go, but a monthly check is only available to those in the system. Instead, Rachel assisted by bringing Christine things she enjoyed, like fashion magazines and crossword puzzles, and healthy foods. Rachel discovered what made Christine feel special.

Befriending Christine was not easy. One day, Rachel went to care for Christine who was in an especially dark place. She ranted as if Rachel was a demon, forgetting who she was, and screamed, "Stay away from me, get away from me." Rachel walked away feeling hurt, questioning her worth and whether or not she was helping. Over the next few days, Rachel's pain and confusion opened a new door. She recognized that her personal pain was caused by the response of a woman who could not receive her attention that day, who was overwhelmed by the voices inside telling her not to trust. By her own declaration, Rachel had an awakening, a transformation. She saw beyond Christine's emotional outburst and no longer needed a loving or even civil response. She saw the soul inside this woman behind her illness and challenging life circumstances. Rachel could live with the personal pain when shunned, allowing herself to walk away because she knew she would return.

After a few years, Rachel learned that Christine's birthday was in June and Rachel made sure they celebrated. Carrot cake and coffee ice cream were Christine's favorites, so right in the middle of the sidewalk on State Street, a party took place. A friend who also lived on the streets joined in. Rachel said Christine was so overjoyed she planned to do it again, but sadly Christine died in her alcove on the street. Rachel was the one to identify her, provided her name to the authorities, and informed them of no known relatives. Christine had called Rachel auntie, not only because Rachel was older but because she cared. She was family.

When asked how she becomes involved with the people she helps, Rachel explains that her spirit tells her which ones to stop for, to care for. Sometimes, she says, she walks past someone, then goes back. She doesn't believe it's her own decision, but her spirit telling her who needs a smile, a kind word, some money, or food. Whatever the history or circumstance of the women she meets, Rachel has learned to approach them with a nonjudgmental attitude, as human beings who deserve love. Rachel says, "I can't imagine never taking a shower, never putting on comforting pajamas and crawling into a clean bed." She has seen the sorrow and suffering, and committed herself to making a difference.

Over time, I learned from one of my neighbors about Rachel's passion for the homeless and that she gives whatever she earns from dog walking to those without homes. Rachel is reticent to share this part of her life. She does not do it for recognition other than the occasional acknowledgment from those she helps. She understands the fear they hold inside from their experiences, the hard knocks of being abused or accosted. Rachel's way is to interact and comfort on a very personal level.

In her life before, high up on the executive ladder at Ford Motor, her life was very different. Did she follow the models of her mother and husband or the spirit within? Now her life is focused on caring for the unloved and banished, walking dogs to gather funds to buy crayons or backpacks. Retirement means many different things, but for Rachel it is about caring. "I think if you give the homeless respect and dignity and food and try to meet their needs, it doesn't matter where they're at." Because many are mentally ill, they often push her care away, which makes the Rachels of this world even more rare.

Tremendous patience is required to understand and forgive, not to push and become defensive, to come back another day. For Rachel, learning the boundaries of others and how to separate her own needs have been steps on the path to learning to care for the homeless. And, as important, she broke from her evangelical rigidity. Rachel faced her pain so she could be there for the pain of others. If her need to be received with kindness was still the demand of her ego, she could not continue. If she needed to be loved in return, she would fail in her efforts.

The successful whittling away of her ego and the insights she gained from Christine and others produced a soldier of mercy. Rachel had to deal with her pain first; any neediness for another's appreciation had to be dissolved. Now she can fulfill her purpose to be there for others, affirming, "I can't imagine living on this planet and realizing that not one person cared for you." This level of compassion is the archetypal work of Chiron the wounded healer, of caring for another's basic needs as an extension of one's own healing. It's been a long path from the child on a farm to controller in a major corporation to retirement as compassionate caregiver. Rachel moved from playing the corporate game to spiritually discovering herself as a helper of homeless women.

REFLECTIONS ON MY JOURNEY
FROM OLDER TO ELDER

1. Did you learn something about yourself in reading Rachel's story? Write about it.

2. How did the challenge of the rage of misunderstanding that Rachel faced when trying to care for the homeless touch you? Did you ever feel similarly rejected when you tried to help someone?

3. What aspects of Rachel's transformation seem marvelous to you?

4. What did you learn from Rachel's joy in celebrating a birthday with a homeless person on the sidewalk? When have you shared with another so unlike yourself? How did it feel?

5. What could you learn from being a healer of the heart of others while your own is frequently broken?

Chapter Nine

ROBBIE

Living in a tenement in Brooklyn, NY, sharing a bedroom with her brother, Robbie didn't have the advantages of children growing up with birds and swings in the backyard. There were few opportunities for outdoor play, but at a very young age, she was sent to sleepaway camp in the Catskills. She remembers a lake and a forest with such tall trees they hid the sky, creating a mysterious den below. Those trees became her friends. That summer she heard the piano for the first time. She may have begun smashing the keys from curiosity and wonder but quickly fell in love with the instrument. At age six, a child's brain picks up languages and builds connections at an amazing rate. Robbie wasn't the next child prodigy, but she discovered and showed her special abilities that summer. It was a very musical camp, with everyone singing and participating in a talent show that allowed her to show an inclination to entertain as well as perform at a keyboard. Sports were also a focus of camp life, and Robbie was introduced to gymnastics, a passion that would continue throughout her school years.

When her family moved to Long Island, Robbie finally had her own bedroom and a new piano. She recalls, "At age seven my grandparents bought me a beautiful baby grand. With this new piano, I got to learn how to play." Her older brother was not around much. Her undemonstrative parents were on their way to getting a divorce and didn't give their daughter much attention. Music became Robbie's sanctuary, her refuge.

The end of high school and her parent's broken marriage marked a different life. Robbie attended a college in Georgia with a "really great, small gymnastics program," but she wasn't prepared for the culture shock of the south, where she was an outsider and a frizzy-haired seventeen-year-old on top of that. The feeling of being a misfit was mended when her dad sent her a keyboard. With this portable piano as her soulmate, she soon formed a tribe of friends to play music with and sing. However, her life in Georgia was cut short when she performed a vault one day and slipped a disc in her back. Her pursuit of gymnastics ended. Returning to New York for surgery was a crisis, not only the pain and slow recovery, but more so the loss of identity she had felt as a gymnast and her love for her physical talent.

Robbie went back to school to study music and English and wrote a number of songs. Through her songwriting, she found a way to express the confusion and heartache that overwhelmed this stage of her life. Success followed, and her first studio recording was a dream come true. She collaborated with a violinist, drummer, and guitarist, singing the harmonies herself. Without gymnastics and with her parents' separation, it was a dark time, even with her music. At nineteen, Robbie chose to enter a psych ward. She had been seeing a therapist one or two hours a week, but it wasn't enough. She wanted "to take care of this" like musician Billy Joel, who admitted himself to a mental hospital at age twenty-one to get rid of his demons and find a focused life where music could be central. While in the hospital, Robbie applied to the Berklee College of Music and was accepted. She studied jazz and music composition, then joined a rock and roll band. She was in the New York music scene for the next twenty years, then bi-coastal, before performing across America on tour.

As she traveled thousands of miles, Robbie's gaze and psyche were intrigued by the decayed frames of old cars and old buildings. Her bass player partner and boyfriend was also a photographer and introduced her to her next passion—photography. Their life together wasn't simply playing music on the road, it was also working on a photographic project, a book of skeletons, abandoned cars, and decaying trees. 1940s cars in the middle of the desert or in an old barn, with light streaming through, prompted her to want to know their stories. Together they embarked on a book of photography that became one of many for Robbie.

The relationship with her photography partner eventually ended. That and the absence of her musical aspirations marked the end of Robbie's interest in the music business. Another crisis was beginning. Robbie found herself back in school, this time a serious and dedicated student of English and journalism who made the dean's list, a difficult achievement for a forty-year-old who had been out of academia for decades. After graduation, diploma in hand, Robbie followed her dream of becoming a professor, sharing her skills and mentoring students on a college campus. But academia didn't offer the access to free thought and opportunities her dreams had imagined. A different career arose in the fashion industry. Robbie tried her journalistic talent at a woman's fashion magazine, but their styles were very different from her tastes and inclinations. The culture of fashion and females competing for a position on the runway with the newest lines didn't resonate.

It became a moment of seeking for Robbie. She had given her inner self to her music, attempting to make a name for herself from the songs she wrote and the live audiences she'd played for, and then had lost the inspiration to continue in that genre. Her days were bleak; she was no longer driven as before to express herself in song before a mic, but no new direction yet pulled her. Academia wasn't her place, and neither was fashion. She experienced the darkness of not knowing. She was lost. A spiritual guru in the verdant nature of Oregon helped her rediscover her source: "This angel of the woods" taught Robbie that we are all connected to the Earth and to each other, that deep inside, we are all joined, and that nature could remind and heal her sense of separation. As Robbie concluded in our interview: "I've learned that we are all connected to all things living. Like the trees so firmly planted in the ground with roots, we continue to grow. And like the seasons, we transition from a time of completion and solitude to a time of the evolution of blooms. We are all on the same journey, just in different places on the path."

Later, Robbie's camera led her to produce a photojournalistic series about places like antique malls, junk yards, and beauty shops. As she explains, "Then I woke up, and the next shoot was a day at the beauty parlor." As an artist at the age of forty-nine, she undertook a major photodocumentary project about women and beauty salons. She didn't regard these women as whimsical but as women who "had lived a life, just a different life from me." She reveals the eye of a photographer in action, joined by her sensitive, compassionate voice. Her documentary took her across the country, interviewing women in their seventies, eighties, and nineties during their weekly beauty parlor appointments. Honoring her mother and grandmother and every woman of the generation that enjoyed the ritual of regular visits to hairdressers, Robbie traces the special friendships that developed over the years. These hairdressers preceded therapists as the ones who allowed women to drop their roles and receive rejuvenation and pampering.

In the book *Beauty and Wisdom*, Robbie portrays women with grace and resiliency, allowing each of them to share words of wisdom about growing older. At fifty, Karen Monroy finally overlooked the physical imperfections of age. The presentation she gave to the world no longer had to be perfect. Now, she says, "I love life anyway. I play more. I laugh more. I love more. I live more. Aging is not the monster we must fear. The monster is the unchallenged marketing machine selling the fountain of youth." Another woman, Florida Scott-Maxwell, explains, "Age puzzles me. I thought it was a quiet time.

My seventies were interesting and fairly serene, but my eighties are passionate. I grow more intense as I age."

The beauty parlor may not be a church, or school, or other institution of cultural value, but it certainly is a community. It is a place where the coverings of femininity are both shed and perpetuated, and in the process of setting curls or dying eyelashes, women support each other. Robbie photographs the unique beauty of older women, their self-acceptance, and their relationships, both with their stylists and each other, all prized through years of return visits. Laura Schultz reminds us, "It is important that we encourage women to value themselves and their unique qualities rather than to base their self-esteem on false notions dictated by others."

Robbie spent years with women who were the ultimate symbols of beauty and reflects that what she discovered was that their souls made them beautiful (or not). Faces that show life and experience, pain and pleasure, wisdom, and weariness, are her choice and statement of "beauty." In giving these various elder women across America an opportunity to have their voices recorded and faces represented in a book that found more than 25,000 Twitter followers, Robbie unexpectedly became a platform for the forgotten and unseen. Through story and portrait, these women are depicted with a vital energy neither daunted nor diminished by age. She captured the intimate moments of becoming undone, of wet heads not yet coiffed, with the trusted partner in the ritual, knowing that the client's appearance would be presentable at the end of her session. Some women arrived for their weekly appointments with a cane or wheelchair, and in that embrace of their strength as females, regardless of age, of their inner confidence as women, they affirmed their commitment to each other. In questioning her own future of being over the hill, of losing her youthful allure, Robbie's crisis in aging became the unconscious catalyst for her book. She showed many readers their futures while reassuring herself that there is strength in aging. Meeting the women of her photojournalistic endeavor, *Beauty and Wisdom*, Robbie documented the independence that waits for those who dare.

As a creative person, Robbie has continued on her path, recently discovering another form of expression: painting on canvas. She shares a day in her life as an artist without formal training undertaking a new medium.

WHY DIDN'T YOU JUST SAY SO?

"This piece was about three or four pieces before this final reincarnation. Needless to say, there are layers and layers of paint that I don't ever think are going to be covered up, but are... repeatedly. I've been working on this canvas for about six months or more...

"During the last stages of this piece, I was creating a landscape scene, one that I had a vision about... with mountains, sky, path... the things that have been inspiring me lately. For the week I worked on it, every day felt more arduous than the last, morphing into work I didn't really like or want or resonate with. There were times I thought I was headed in the right direction only to wind up at another dead end.

"As it sometimes happens, all the prior 'mistakes' were the perfect underlining for what was about to happen.

"After feeling completely frustrated with this painting and myself, I said out loud to it, 'If you just wanted to be an abstract, why didn't you just say so?!!' I haphazardly grabbed paint and covered most of the canvas... did a little technique that I use and... was blown away by the ease in which this abstract 'created itself.'

"What most painters know, I think, is that the harder we 'try' to contrive something the more of a losing battle it becomes since the creative process truly stems from somewhere other than ourselves... at least, that's what I believe to be true for me.

"So when 'I' got out of the way... 'Here Comes the Sun' is what came through...pun intended."

-Robbie Kaye

Robbie has a relentless drive, whatever the medium, to explore and share her self-discovery. Her subjects are often trees, many trees, from a previous fascination with solitary oak trees. There is usually a path of some sort through a forest with a single bird somewhere. As a human being on this vast planet, Robbie is returning to her earliest memories at camp. In her words, "I'm coming full circle. My appreciation of nature has been so healing for me. It's always been a place to clear my mind…the trees have endured just like the women of the beauty parlors." Their commitment to live and thrive after earthquakes and through devastations of flood, fire, and storm reinforces how we, too, endure as humans.

Whether composing a song, a photo story, or an oil painting, Robbie shares her inner turmoil, her pains, and joys. Aging offers us the gift of acceptance and not having to be in control. In closing, I offer Robbie's words and what the women of *Beauty and Wisdom* taught her: "To never give up, follow your dreams. You can attain whatever you want at any age." Robbie hopes to inspire other women to start new careers at any age, to pursue what brings them joy. Her numerous life crises blossomed into an unstoppable creative force, manifesting itself in musical notes, photographic poetry, and now mixed media paintings embedded with crystals. Robbie's work has a haunting and luminous aspect, calling the viewer or listener inside herself, inside her soul.

The healing power of such an artist is unmistakable, joining viewer with nature, interconnecting the elves of the woods from childhood fantasies to the crystalline harshness of the present. As her words encourage, "Your heart is the epicenter of the universe. Open it up and send resounding love to all that need healing, for we all need healing."

Reflections on My Journey from Older to Elder

1. Do you remember having a childhood curiosity for an artistic pursuit, either with a paintbrush, musical instrument, or physical activity? What was that like?

2. Were you supported in this? Or did you play alone at this new activity or entertainment? What caused you to continue, or if you didn't, why not?

3. Have you been in a relationship that sustained your creativity? How did you transition out of the relationship when it ended? Or are you struggling now to carry on your creative work without a partner?

4. Would you like to explore writing or artwork now? If you had the time, which direction would you explore first? What is preventing you?

Chapter Ten

JILLIAN

For most of her life, Jillian felt she didn't belong on this planet. She was born into a dysfunctional family marked by anger and chaos. Her parents divorced and her father later found his way to sobriety, but her formative years had already filled her with fear and blame. Her mother used her as a scapegoat, framing her daughter as the one who had created the lack of love and harmony, even though she was only an innocent child. Jillian's disruptive childhood extended to a sense of not belonging. When she was old enough, she left home.

She was not career-oriented and sought the path of drugs and alcohol frequented by many in their twenties. To financially support her life choices, she managed restaurants, a daunting position for a young gal, sober or not. Even then, Jillian remembers searching for meaning, trying to fill the empty hole. Warmth flooded her body when she first tasted alcohol. She felt empowered. In her drunken state of grandiosity, she asked herself, "Is it God that has saved me?" She experienced delusions, imagining herself free of limiting realities. But she was not so grand, and her life crumbled. At that time, she also started suffering from the pain of psoriatic arthritis. Sleep evaded her, and addiction ensued. Alcohol had been the drug her father chose, and it became Jillian's drug. Her lack of sobriety ended her employment and all she had built in her life to that point. Hallucinations and psychosis replaced managing restaurants. She lost the ability to take care of herself.

For a long time, darkness excluded hope or anything close to joy. As her world fell apart, Jillian felt separate from everything. Drinking to excess, she recalls many terrifying nights with demons taunting her about her worthlessness, frightening her "out of her wits" without a helpful ally anywhere. Fear took over. Then one night, in a hospital emergency room, she almost died. She woke up surrounded by unfamiliar male doctors and an occasional female nurse trying to save her life. She had been poisoned by alcohol. Lying on the table in the ICU, Jillian "saw a light above her…and knew that she was going to be okay." She was finished with her bouts of drinking and spent the next five months in a rehabilitation facility.

The recovery program helped Jillian regain some physical well-being but not the spiritual strength she so desperately sought. Years of drinking and nightlife left her totally alone and unable to reassemble the pieces of her life. Her anger at her mother and father, now separated, created a barrier to starting over with her parents. Her behaviors were blunt and coarse from the demands of survival as a street person, and she turned away any potential new acquaintances. She yearned to discover the meaning of the words she received as a youngster that had once told her she was here for a purpose. She felt guided by a voice within or perhaps outside herself, an angel, she didn't know, but a guide had spoken to her way back in her childhood.

Jillian discovered an online advertisement for a school in New Zealand. The look of joy and freedom on the face of the young woman in the photograph showed the new life that Jillian sought, a gloriously different world. This girl represented a bright future of opportunity and a hopeful spirit Jillian still knew inside. She researched the school and discovered it was led by a man named Kent Ferguson, but the school across the ocean in New Zealand had closed. Jillian was determined and found out that Kent had started the Santa Barbara Middle School beforehand.

How to find this school with a girl swinging from a tree on the other side of the globe? As a not so recently released patient, Jillian took on the job of a professional detective, driven by a vision. The sister school in Santa Barbara, also mentioned in the magazine, was key. Jillian was persistent in chasing her dream and began emailing Kent. In the beginning, he didn't respond to her crazy-sounding messages that were far different from the usual inquiries parents made for their pre-teen children. Jillian didn't know the words for what she was seeking, but she was enchanted by that girl in the ad, by an inner dream of also being a happy child in a special school in a faraway place.

Eventually, Kent and Jillian met in New Zealand. She arrived dressed in fatigues and hiding her face, appearing more like a boorish boy than a young woman. Together, they visited the grounds of Kent's former school. It was an old estate with thirty-four bedrooms that had been his to live in as headmaster. Both seemed to be chasing a fleeting dream, not of romantic partnership—the age difference and fragility of Jillian's psyche did not permit that—but a higher purpose. She sought the stability and promise of belonging while he sought a partner. Neither yet understood their different needs, but they pursued their separate discoveries for the next fifteen years.

Their path took them to New Mexico, where Kent owned a piece of land amid three Native American reservations and adjoining a Tibetan stupa. It was a magical backdrop for an unusual and very spiritual partnership. Jillian and Kent did not battle but also didn't completely understand one another. He was very much a headmaster of children just discovering themselves and a seeker himself of a deeper spiritual path, while she was learning how to live as a grown-up with rudimentary social skills. Where they might meet as persons after finding each other in the airport after her flight to New Zealand is a dark mystery. How could they even speak to each other, she coming from the streets and rehab, and he from a career encouraging children to sit on a log and listen to teachers? His educational style was unusual and exciting for youngsters, but Jillian wasn't a youngster and had already lived a desperate life as an adult. They survived in an old van and embarked on the construction of a bale home with a composting toilet. Her search for personal meaning had begun. Jillian admitted to Kent later that she needed him "to teach her to be a human." Her years of alcoholism had taken away whatever she had known.

Jillian realized that moving ahead with her life meant starting over. She had "to unlearn and relearn, to replace the conditioned life responses of her recent years." Recovery from addiction to alcohol in Alcoholics Anonymous requires steps one and two: "We admitted we were powerless over alcohol and our lives were unmanageable. We turned our will and our lives over to a higher power as we understand it, to restore us to sanity." Jillian chose not to follow her father's dogmatic approach to sober living but intuitively grasped her need to find a spiritual path. Kent represented this power for Jillian, not as her guru or God, but a spiritual entity, a force of good. He is almost twenty years older, so he has some fatherly aspects simply by virtue of age. But it was his lifetime of encouraging and channeling the vital energies of youngsters that formed the strength of character Jillian needed. She had come from the terror of drug-induced craziness, and the school leader represented order and a pathway forward.

Nature in the desolate land of New Mexico also offered the spiritual: bountiful stars above, wildlife emerging from behind the bushes, the chatter of birds. Jillian wasn't alone, but part of her kept seeking something more. The friendship with Kent was strange to her. Was he her employer or father, teacher, or enemy? In the beginning, she and Kent lived more like brother and sister.

Social life was limited to the Native Americans on nearby reservations and occasional trips to the nearest community an hour away for groceries and supplies. Jillian learned to use her computer to find answers. Her questions were the same that other younger people were asking about their culture and the challenges of civil injustice and ecological collapse. This generation, born in the eighties and nineties, was considered by some a new breed of human—the indigo children with creative and empathetic abilities to help heal the planetary sickness. Jillian considers herself an indigo child who chose to come into this world to help heal the planet and all sentient beings.

Indigos, some believe, were the predominant (more than 90 percent) children under age ten in 1999. Many of these magical children were misdiagnosed with ADHD or ADD because of their inability to sit still or concentrate. According to many therapists and teachers who dealt with them, indigo children showed similar characteristics. Likewise, parents were confused and frustrated by their inability to handle such independent forces they had brought into the world. One guidance counselor advised, "Indigo children come into this life with self-respect and an unshakeable understanding that they are children of God...nothing turns an indigo off faster than parents who do not earn their child's respect but who instead give away their power and parental responsibility to the child." It doesn't matter if science proves that this is a special a type of being or if it's a hypothetical tribe because learning about them explained Jillian's uniqueness to herself.

As she moved away from her old world, she felt drawn to her mother, to befriending the woman who gave her life, and to understanding her misfortune in choosing the alcoholic man she had married. Perhaps the Catholic upbringing and the guardian angel of her confirmation brought her back. Jillian doesn't know but is glad that the warmth of spirit she discovered in New Mexico eclipsed the harsh recollections of New England. She felt a reconciliation and followed through with weekly, then daily, phone calls to her mother.

She realized that not only her mother but many people fear death. Jillian does not. Death is not an enemy because she has come so close to it. As she began to reenter a relationship with her family, healing the broken bonds, her mother shared her fear of talking about dying. This started Jillian on her path as a death doula. Her near-death experiences showed her that there is an afterlife, and she wanted to share this with her mother.

Until recently, modern death practices in America and Europe only set forth protocols of last rites, funeral, and burial or cremation, excluding sacred preparations that other cultures historically provided. The ancient Egyptians had elaborate funerary practices, which they believed were necessary to ensure transition to the afterlife. These rituals included mummifying the body, casting magic spells, and burial with specific grave goods thought to be needed in the next life. They regarded death as a temporary interruption rather than a cessation of life. The Buddhists have the *Tibetan Book of the Dead* to guide the soul. A religious leader might read from this book for forty-five days to ensure that the soul finds its passage to a felicitous rebirth. Native Americans believe that their shamans guide the spirit in their inner journeys. By entering the inner world, they can accompany and travel beside the newly departed.

As previously mentioned, author and psychiatrist Elisabeth Kübler-Ross, who taught of stages of grief, also brought awareness to the possibility of assisting the dying in a compassionate and spiritual way from this life to the beyond. Her words continue to guide hospice volunteers in America and Europe today. Shared death experiences, being present for the moments between living and dying, became Jillian's passion, and she sought guidance in how best to be there for those who requested help in their final stage of life. She found a teaching center in Colorado and traveled there to learn how to become a death doula. Each doula has unique gifts to honor and assist in the transition during one's final moments.

Jillian believes one of her life purposes is to be there for others as they begin their next life, to be present for these moments, experiencing the bright light of joy. It was neither frightening nor painful for her. Some may begin assistance on the dying path sooner, helping the family as well as the individual to accept or find closure. Sometimes a death doula may cross over with the dying, assisting as a guide. This was Jillian's special gift. Although her mother died during COVID when hospitals didn't allow families to enter, Jillian knows that her telephone conversations with her mother were much deeper than a wire transmission of sound. As a result of the deep bonding between reunited mother and daughter at an energetic level, Jillian knew she had assisted her mother in transitioning with serenity.

Jillian's unique tale of recovery in the enchanted land of New Mexico gives hope to those who struggle. In her words, "It's a lifetime of discovering yourself and not wanting to discover yourself and facing your fears and your lessons…and realizing that what we are doing here is school." Many teachers are available to seekers on the internet, and even a student in the desolate Eden of New Mexico can connect with them. Jillian has found several wisdom sharers to help her through periods of unknowing. She "went to hell and back" with alcohol to be ready for them. Addiction was her path to help others heal.

Jillian went through a dark night of the soul for years, lost in a world where she didn't feel she belonged and suffering from physical pain that didn't stop. She sought the return of a voice that once told her she had a purpose and a guide for her soul. She was shown her gift of assisting the dying in crossing over to their next life in peace. Even her mother, whom she had battled for most of her life, sought Jillian's wisdom in her final days. According to the *Tibetan Book on Death and Dying*, fear in the face of death is the gateway to the most demonic of visions for the journey ahead. To find peace and acceptance before that final journey may be the most healing of all lifetime gifts.

Reflections on My Journey from Older to Elder

1. At some point in your life, have you struggled, like Jillian, with a sense of not belonging? How did you find greater meaning and purpose? Did you identify a group of like-minded individuals who inspired you or helped you understand why you felt adrift? Were you able to bring new ideas or practices into your life that grounded you? What were they?

2. Describe your family life and childhood. Are there areas of your upbringing that were difficult? Do you feel resolved about them, or can you see how you may want to explore them? Do you see qualities that have persisted from your youth that you wish to change? How can you begin to let go of these negative patterns, thoughts, or behaviors?

3. How would you describe your relationship with your parents? If you are estranged from them, do you feel the desire to reconnect like Jillian? Write about it.

4. Can you recall reading about or seeing something like the school Jillian found that felt like a flash of intuition? Did you become deeply engaged, possibly obsessed, with finding it? How did it affect your life direction?

Chapter Eleven

JANE GOODALL

Her early life as Valerie Jane was a childhood in England; her adult life as Jane Goodall is a traveling advocate for the chimpanzees at the edge of extinction, their homelands disappearing. She dedicated her life to answering their call for help. According to Dale Peterson, Jane's lifelong collaborator, it may have been her father's gift of a stuffed chimpanzee at her first birthday that formed her life. This life-size cuddly buddy was much more than a toy for a child with an imagination such as Jane's. This stuffed chimpanzee named Jubilee moved with the family and was always at the front of her collection of stuffed animals, but in her own words it was her "closest companion Rusty that so-intelligent black mongrel" who played an important role in defining what and whom she became.

I did not personally interview Jane but am sharing insights from her writings and information written about her.

We get to know Jane through *Jane Goodall: The Woman Who Redefined Man*, a biography by Dale Peterson. According to Peterson, World War II didn't affect the family much in the beginning, though Jane's father joined the troops and her mother helped stretch finances by working in a canteen every afternoon. During teatime one afternoon, five-year-old Jane disappeared, sending not only the nanny and her mother out searching for her but also the remaining staff and villagers. Finally, a soldier appeared with young Jane. When asked where she'd been until nightfall, Jane replied, "Watching a hen." She'd been watching a hen lay an egg! Jane already understood the necessity of patience when observing the natural behaviors of wild animals. Her prize? "I saw a round white object gradually protruding from the feathers between her legs. It got bigger. Suddenly she gave a wiggle—and plop—it landed on the straw." It was Jane's first research project.

After her primary education, Jane's future didn't include going to university due to finances, so she entered secretarial school, which eventually led to the realization of her childhood dream of being in Africa. She became secretary to Louis Leakey, whose work in Africa on the discovery of early man was leading him to world renown. Leakey also had an interest in primates. When he received funding for his chimpanzee research project, Jane was in a position to take over. He was determined to place a researcher in the remotest of places, knowing the position demanded an ability to endure both isolation and boredom as well as danger. The passion and curiosity of his untrained secretary more than compensated for her lack of scientific background.

Jane's first six months in Gombe, Tanzania, provided unexpected challenges. In the jungle, she was frustrated with the chimps' shyness and with the "watchers," the country park officials demanded she take with her into the jungle each day. They couldn't keep up. Though natives, they lacked Jane's youthfulness and interest. Eventually, she left them behind and forged on alone, ever more eager as a few of the chimpanzees appeared to be unafraid of her. She walked in the jungle as one of them, and they started to accept her. Previous researchers had attempted to hide and observe from a distance, or in the case of the Japanese man from Kyoto University, plant a sugar cane plantation to draw them near. Jane singularly became part of their habitat. She followed them into their forest home. The chimps of Gombe weren't animals but friends, sentient beings with personalities.

Jane told Steve Paulson in an interview for the Salon website, "They'd never seen a white ape before, and they were horrified. They vanished into the bushes. Fortunately, one of them—I named him David Greybeard—lost his fear before the others and came to my camp, where he found some bananas. And it was because of him that the others gradually began to lose their fear. So it was as though he helped me open a door into a magic world."

After sixteen months observing their everyday lives, Jane announced new findings about chimpanzees—they ate meat and used tools. Her observation of a monkey using a twig to capture a termite changed primatology. Further documentation of mother-child behavior and male dominance behavior gave Gombe Research Center world renown and Jane a busy schedule of attending conferences and giving keynote speeches. Jane was not a scientist or highly accepted by the scientific community. She rejected common conventions such as identifying the chimpanzees by number, instead choosing to give her participants names. Granting identities to chimpanzees after following them in the wild for many months was very different from putting them in cages and studying them.

According to Peterson's biography, Jane discovered habits and personalities verified by personal observation. These observations were game changers and overturned the rigid scientific beliefs regarding monkeys and man. And they came from a female untrained by academia until she was admitted to Cambridge to earn her PhD. With the equivalent of a high school diploma, Jane, the young female with a blonde ponytail, gained a global reputation. Researchers came from around the world to hear her speak, and her papers were widely published. Jane practiced and taught a scientific approach that combined traditional European ethology with her intuitive ways of thinking. Her work remains central to the achievement of twentieth- and twenty-first-century primatology.

But who is Dr. Jane Goodall? Basically, she's a young woman who was paid to watch monkeys in Africa. Watching involved long days of seeking, of climbing steep mountains to find these monkeys, and hours more alone in a tent writing her findings. She didn't try to make friends with the monkeys as pets but identified them individually, observing mothers caring for their babies, playing with them and reprimanding them, staying with them, and protecting them for many years. Jane was married twice, and both her husbands, Hugo and Derek, were involved for a time in her research; the first was a photographer, and the second a Tanzanian park director. I suspect both became jealous of her fame and unwilling to share her with the world.

Interestingly, it may have been a plane crash that both propelled Jane to end her first marriage and enter the second. The reality of her near-death experience may also have influenced her later move from research scientist to activist. Recognition of her mortality helped Jane ally with the cause of preventing the mortality of her chimpanzees in a fast-changing country on the African continent. Population and internal politics, poverty, and warfare pushed against their habitat, specifically the research station in Gombe that Jane had dedicated her life to. A kidnapping by Marxist rebels of five students from her center exacerbated the split between Jane and her husband, Hugo, and the American embassy and Tanzanian government. Ultimately, ransom funds freed the hostages, and Laurent Kabila, the leader of the kidnappers, drove the president of what was then Zaire out of office and off the continent, thereby becoming president of the African nation. Protecting the chimpanzees did not show up in mission statements for the new regimes. This traumatic affair and the loss of her husband may have been the turning point in Jane's life, propelling her to become an activist. In Jane's own words, "For me Africa has always been the ruling force of my life, I suppose. Now it is even more than that. Lots of things seem to have fallen into shape after being nearly dead—you know, you suddenly realize that it could happen (death, I mean) at any moment." Her biographer concludes that after the publicity of the crash, she agreed with Derek that they should divorce their spouses and marry each other. I propose that the combination of challenging events in Jane's life at this time might be considered a crisis and cause of transformative change that we have been documenting for self-discovery in later-life females.

Committed to saving the habitat and home of the chimpanzees and apes, Jane founded the Jane Goodall Institute, establishing a fund to assist where needed. She personally embarked on a media campaign between 1987 and 1990 to fund the institute and increase public awareness of the desperate condition of the diminishing wildlife being sold for food or starved by the lack of habitat as human settlements encroached on their territory. In addition to publishing her book *Through a Window, My Thirty Years with the Chimpanzees of Gombe*, she scheduled hundreds of media interviews and was key to completing six national television productions in North America and Europe.

Jane's involvement extended to helping children help the environment. She founded Roots and Shoots in 1991. Her passionate concern for animals and their habitat was contagious. She inspired youth to begin their own projects, and now in preschool to university classrooms in more than 140 countries, young people participate in Roots and Shoots clubs. More than 150,000 club members are empowered to work on environmental, conservation, and humanitarian issues of their choosing. Jane celebrated her seventieth birthday at a party in Los Angeles with giant dove of peace puppets raised high and swaying gracefully by three Roots and Shoots youngsters. Her *Book of Hope, A Survival Guide for Trying Times*, encapsulates her philosophy and life mission. Her message is that we can continue as a species on this planet only if we commit to caring. The resilience of nature, along with the power of young people, bring hope to this endeavor.

Sanctuaries for chimpanzees initiated by the Jane Goodall Institute and the youth projects supported by Roots and Shoots are tackling a relatively small problem in the total demise of the Earth's previous bounty. However, Jane's example in rising to solve these problems and in educating and motivating through Skype, Zoom, and other platforms continues to inspire. Now in her eighties, she hasn't given up before the accelerating pace of global malaise. The chimpanzee population in her Gombe park has declined because the surrounding people are poor and hungry. Jane's teams from the institute recognized the local people as partners and inquired about what would make their lives better. It was health and their children's education, so that is where the institute began. Their mission is to save the chimpanzees by improving the lives of the people.

When asked where she gets her strength to continue, Jane wrote, "I sort of open my mind to some kind of outside force…I just relax and decide to appeal to the source of the hidden strength, to that spiritual power that seems to have sent me on this mission." Her unfailing faith and curiosity led her from watching a hen lay an egg in England to the forests of Africa observing chimpanzees to speaker's podiums around the world. Her advice to us all from her book: "There is hope for our future—for the health of our planet, our societies, and our children. But only if we get together and join forces."

REFLECTIONS ON MY JOURNEY FROM OLDER TO ELDER

1. Can you describe the crises of Jane's life and the paths she found to a new self? For example, would you consider the loss of her second husband a catalyst to her new passion for the habitat of chimpanzees? How so? How did the crisis of the kidnapping transform her?

2. If you could have a conversation with Jane Goodall, what questions would you ask her?

3. Was her beginning dream anything like her dreams in late life? What do you think propelled her to her later levels of global passion?

4. How does Jane's life inspire the children to join the Roots and Shoots groups? Where do you think Jane got the inspiration to lead children as well as save animals in zoos? Do you remember times in your own life when you were able to help others? What motivated you?

5. Even if the actions you listed above seem small and insignificant to others, can you feel the different person you grew to be from them? Do you now feel more a part of the world, as if your small place is one of kindness?

Chapter Twelve

BEING REPLACES DOING IN A STATE OF CONTINUOUS AWAKENING

The prospect of a new life in older age is linked to the possibility of transcending the self. Transcendence implies a cosmic joining, a soulful connection, with a love for self and community. In research for his gerotranscendence, a developmental theory of aging, Lars Tornstam introduced a concept of the older as a transcendent individual who is less self-occupied and more apt to choose meditative times of solitude. This is similar to the wisdom of Ram Dass who guided listeners to lift the veil between layers of consciousness. Gerotranscendence proposes a stage of development that includes a new understanding of reality, reaching beyond the ordinary of the everyday to transcend boundaries. Tornstam and Dass write of deepened spirituality, with higher capacities of heightened intuition, as potential characteristics of late life. Cosmic communion is a term both teachers use.

While Eric Erikson's long-standing theory on psychological development identifies only the possibility of wisdom as a characteristic of the late stage of life, Swedish gerontologist Tornstam takes the next step by directly integrating wisdom within the aging process. "Erikson," Tornstam writes, "as do others who talk vaguely about wisdom, intuitively comes close to what our studies find as satisfaction potentials in late life without… comprehending the necessary shift to enlightened maturity as a flow of cosmic energy replacing materialistic and rational perspective." Where Erikson defines ego-integrity as the end stage of human development after successful transitions through the crises of each stage and an integration of elements in the life past, gerotranscendence focuses on an inner and outward direction toward the future. As an elder myself, I find the new state of awareness given to me as a gift from somewhere above or within that directs me to acts of compassion. I gave up trying to control my world or compete to prove I could. I entered a new realm of trust, of knowing I am loved without doing a thing. I am living in a world of joy instead of judgment, of comfort in purely being.

Development toward gerotranscendence proposes progress through the passageways of unknowing to the transformation of becoming an elder while emphasizing the possible role of life crises as catalysts. Tornstam explains that "life crises may contain the *kinetic* energy that make the development towards gerotranscendence accelerate." The role of crises in one's life may be not only the power of the upheaval itself but also a double effect in causing one to question a previous concept of reality. Death of a close relative, for example, may undermine ideas of immortality, the notion that it will never happen to me, and create a new foundation of beliefs. In some older individuals, there is a new acceptance of life and death. A decrease in self-centeredness and an increase in self-transcendence are observed as a shift from egotism to altruism.

From his interviews with aging individuals, Tornstam began to observe a cosmic dimension to aging. Certain individuals achieve a new acceptance of life and death, discovering hidden aspects of self, both good and bad, and a decrease in self-centeredness leading to self-transcendence. Growing into the gerotranscendent individual entails a redefinition of the self and re-engagement with the world. Self-interest will only obscure the spiritual path and any possibility of transformation. This paradigm shift from scientific to spiritual also informs the writings of Carl Jung and Albert Einstein. When the self merges into a cosmic reality, you are held as if by the Universe. A beautiful testimony to this unity appears in a book by Dass and his dear friend, Mirabai Bush. She writes, "Being with (Ram), I realize again and again, that there is no separation between life, death, cats, grieving parents—they are part of a seamless whole." Reality has permeable boundaries, or no boundaries, once we become an elder.

Gerotranscendence is a development possibility, a seed that needs to be watered, but in today's society, Tornstam writes, "we probably lack much of the proper watering, which means that the proportion of individuals who reach high degrees of gerotranscendence is quite small." Tornstam observed that a bridge to gerotranscendence might be a quality of experiencing nature or music, either becoming more profound or more emotional. In one interview, a seventy-seven-year-old man said that a barrier between music and emotion had been broken down. Tornstam's team interpreted this individual's comments as transcending the barrier to a deeper emotional response. Increasing emotionality is a symptom of disintegrating personality in situations, music, or nature that are relatively free from boundaries.

In 2013, Rev. John Robinson, author, interfaith minister, and psychologist, introduced the concept of conscious aging, a radical reconceptualization of aging, with his book *Aging as a Mystical Experience*. He produced a blueprint for the enlightened elder of the twenty-first century. In this largely uncharted stage of psychological and spiritual development, when an individual is often most able to evolve and give back, aging can become a mystical experience. Aging is a "disguise that hides an amazing and profound process of human spiritual evolution." According to Robinson, aging represents a natural transformation of self and consciousness. The events and processes of aging, from changing bodies and fading identities, are an initiation. We surrender the self we knew and this process of loss, as the mystics tell us, contains the elements of enlightenment. What is left when the ego dissolves is consciousness itself. Living in a sea of consciousness, we receive reassurance from a larger presence that comforts us and grants us spontaneous insights. For some individuals, this loss of personal boundaries is a joining with the Earth and the entire Cosmos.

From this new consciousness as elders, we can change the world. Rev. Robinson calls this mystical activism. In Robinson's theory, mystical activism is a new consciousness. "The mystical realizations can transform our aging if we are willing to descend into the unfathomable depths of inner space" and use our beliefs and life experiences to inform our awareness and actions. Again and again, Robinson invites us to seek the direct experience of God within ourselves and the natural world as a means to "remediate the suffering of humans and other life forms." Our inner awakening allows us to perceive the world in sensory wonder. The veil of thought and belief no longer obscures our awareness. Mystical activism integrates our spiritual awakening with our lifetime of wisdom to serve the world anew.

Self-transformation is essential for becoming a gerotranscendent being or a mystical activist. Both Tornstam and Robinson describe satisfaction in late life resulting from separation from mid-life values of activity and productiveness. A new perspective of the self in union replaces the lifelong construction of self as separate or superior. In Robinson's words, "we work to dissolve the self-idea into the thought-free consciousness of the mystic as we release our entanglements from the imagined problems and emotions that previously bound us." The process of development in the second half of life is a reversal of the first half, in many ways breaking the personal abilities considered strong and essential for success.

In his writings, Dass describes later life as a period of accepting change. "The nature of aging has to do with change. Old age trains you for change—change in your body, change in your memory, change in your relationships, change in your family and social role—all leading to death." On the other hand, he reassures these changes have another side. "The clamor of the ego calms." Wisdom and contentment begin to come forth, and a new consciousness emerges. Contentment is "one of the mindsets you use to direct your consciousness toward oneness…True contentment is an attitude of the soul rather than of the ego or personality."

We may be entering the transcendent realm of the spirit, a consciousness different from the everyday when we step into the experience of being an elder. Transcendence and cosmic consciousness are concepts that imply an individual's ability to move into another reality in which the world feels different. Before, when still locked in pursuit of some gain in the material world, satisfying our egos, or our fears that we might fail, we could see only a limited world. Now we enter a world of continuous awakening. Dass talks of breaking down boundaries so that we come together in oneness. "You are standing on the beach, you put down your shoes and your ego, and then you dive in." In our elder years, we may gradually fall into gerotranscendence, slowly joining in the oneness of being.

As we ask less of ourselves, we find more time and new joy. This time to listen allows us to hear and appreciate music, the birds, and the words of loved ones. A new world of wonderment opens. Compassion is another gift of wisdom, compassion for yourself, compassion for others, compassion for the world. If we return to the myth of Chiron, we also return to the dictum, healer, heal thyself and thus the world. Wisdom takes the "non-action" of sharing the flow of new consciousness, creative awakening, and new healing modalities. We, as elders, become healers by being awakened and extending this gift to others. We are wounded healers like Chiron.

Jane Goodall frames her experience of growing into a deeper relationship with all living beings when she describes, "All the time I was getting closer to animals and nature, and as a result, closer to myself and more and more in tune with the spiritual power that I felt all around. For those who have experienced the joy of being alone with nature there is really little need for me to say much more; for those who have not, no words of mine can even describe the powerful, almost mystical knowledge of beauty and eternity that come, suddenly, and all unexpected."

Becoming an elder is a dynamic process that both redefines one's sense of self and requires an open acceptance of change. Dass asks, "Can you live in the presence of change, even enjoy the changes—work with the changes, become an elder? Allow the changes and delight in them and look for the wisdom inherent in each change rather than resisting them?" When we no longer know ourselves as doing something but as being aware of something, a sense of oneness takes over. In a new consciousness, reality has permeable boundaries. A state of continuous awakening is within.

"A Place to Sit," a Sufi prayer from the fifteenth century, teaches:

Don't go outside your house to see the flowers.

My friend, don't bother with that excursion.

Inside your body there are flowers.

One flower has a thousand petals.

That will do for a place to sit.

Sitting there you will have a glimpse of beauty

Inside the body and out of it,

Before gardens and after gardens.

-Kabir

REFLECTIONS ON MY JOURNEY
FROM OLDER TO ELDER

Your new awareness of eldership may include a deeper feeling of belonging and of having a more purposeful self.

1. Do you feel a deeper connection to nature? Describe the new perceptions and feelings.

2. Do you feel more empathic toward others? More compassionate toward the pain of the world? Toward yourself? If so, in what ways?

3. Are you feeling more serene, at peace inside? What in your daily life gives you a calmness and feeling of connection?

4. As you reflect on the previous you—homemaker, career professional—are you feeling more distant from her, aware that you've separated from her? How so?

5. Identify some of the differences in yourself now compared to the person before your crisis.

6. Are you more able to accept the changes in your physical body or in your financial status or social position? Think of several instances that show how you have accepted the hand that fate has given you, that your inner sage guides you toward.

7. In what ways are you an advocate of life and thus an ally of the young? Do your new way of being and sense of purpose support the healing of others and of nature?

Your journey has brought you to being an elder and
knowing you have wisdom to share.

Chapter Thirteen

CONCLUSION

The Lakota Prayer to Wakan Tanka speaks to the women on their paths shared in the chapters of this book:

Teach me how to trust my heart
Teach me to trust my mind
Teach me to trust my inner knowing,
Teach me to trust the senses of my body
So that I may enter my Sacred Space
And love beyond my fear.
And thus walk in balance.

After facing the darkness and arising in their new selves, the females interviewed were able to act based on the truth of their hearts. In every case, their passions directed them to serve others from an inner knowing, a spiritual messenger.

The healing Chiron archetype and ancient myth help us to see more clearly, to know the story of each of these women as wounded healers. We agree with John Robinson's twenty-first-century aging as an entirely new stage of life, a mystical experience for some. The call to face the demons of darkness, to undergo a rite of transformation, usually must precede the glorious possibility of later life. Some are distracted by modernity, by all the entertainment venues that call an individual away, the drugs and alcohol that may make the path too fuzzy to see, make the person too weak to take the steps ahead.

Losses are guaranteed at all stages of life, and facing death is a last opportunity for each of us to prepare for the final moments, but many are too afraid. We are frightened of the steady dissolution of social constructs that define us and of the physical bodies that held us, of our abilities to do what we once did. Woundedness, for these, remains as a kind of victimology, not as a doorway to elder as healer. Grown-ups may not grow up, may not follow an inner path of spirit.

I hope this workbook will guide women to take steps to find their path to passion in their lives. The women who shared their stories give examples of very different lives to very different soulful, later passions. In different ways, each is inspirational. We may not feel drawn to be death doulas or even to make paintings of trees with tiny birds, but our inner need to express ourselves and serve others comes when we have moved beyond the first half of life. Now we are free—having succeeded in creating a family or career, perhaps both—and can answer the call within. Moving out of personal shadows that try to stop us is a tough job, tougher than any before. We weren't given a map. Late life never included these added decades.

As women, we are survivors with a vision of those who have gone before us, whether from a rough childhood on a ranch or alcoholism in a very strict Catholic family in New England. Whatever our beginning, another chapter awaits. Our lives may not look exciting to others as we follow our soul's calling, but we've moved beyond caring for the judgment of others, including ourselves. Later life is liberated. Our guide is within, and energy is found to enjoy life in some meaningful way. The handcuffs of ego have been weakened or are gone altogether.

In some way, each of the stories of the interviewees ended with an ability to move beyond personal boundaries. Apparently, the loosening of ego was matched by an ability to enter the reality of others. Whether as therapist into the world of analysis or as primate watcher into the caring hearts of others around the world, these women extended themselves well beyond their previous selves. In their elder years they essentially became much more: a companion to the homeless able to find them, or a death doula able to cross over with the dying. Ram Dass says that these individuals have entered a spiritual state that is more inclusive and are motivated by love. Love as an energy in his theology is very similar to the mutual empathy that the Wellesley researchers wrote about as the energetic component females have in relationship as a goal of development. I would go further to say that these women have learned to leave their given reality to pass into the reality of another to better serve them. Passing through the veil that separates us is a possibility when ego boundaries become weaker, as is frequently the case with age. Each woman interviewed went through a crisis and dark night of the soul and emerged renewed and inspired.

The women in the previous chapters all exhibit a fervent faith in the causes they are passionate about. For each, it was a development in late life that was essentially a new identity, a newfound self after dissolution of their previous personas. Whether they are guided by their spirits or simply by a vigorous life force that nature endows each of us with from birth, we can see that later life for women can offer inspiring gifts for those who don't waver or fall on their journey. Like Chiron, they are wounded heroes who came to be healers, wounded first, then living in the reality of interconnectedness. These women separately showed their responses to Carl Jung and John Robinson's question: How could aging be the crowning achievement of life? In their time of crises, they walked through the doorway to the darkness and came out to be crowned with new meaning in their lives and new life energy.

NOTES

Chapter One

- Delehanty, Hugh, "Native American Novelist."
- Miller, Jean Baker, *Toward a New Psychology of Women.*
- Jordan, Judith, "The Meaning of Mutuality," 11.
- Harjo, Joy, *Poet Warrior, a Memoir,* 187.
- Thomas, William H., *What are Old People For?,* 94.

Chapter Two

- Hollis, James, *Finding Meaning in the Second Half of Life,* 9.
- Peers, E. Allison, trans & ed, *Interior Castle, St. Teresa of Avila.*
- Keating, Thomas, *Invitation to Love,* 51.

- Moody, Harry R., and David Carroll, *Five Stages of the Soul.*
- Wikman, Monika, *Pregnant Darkness*, 27.
- Wikman, Monika, *Pregnant Darkness*, xix.
- Dass, Ram with Rameshwar Das, *The Polishing Mirror*, 100.

Chapter Three

- Leder, Drew, *Spiritual Passages*, 21.
- Keating, Thomas, *Intimacy with God*, 1.
- May, Gerald, *The Dark Night of the Soul*, 73.
- May, Gerald, *The Dark Night of the Soul*, 83.
- Baker, Willa Blythe, *The Wakeful Body*, 47.
- Arrien, Angeles, *The Second Half of Life*, 129.
- Kübler-Ross, Elisabeth, *On Death and Dying, 110.*
- Meade, Michael, *Fate and Destiny*, 233.

Chapter Four

- Erikson & Erikson, (1998), Borysenko (1996, 1999), Stone Center (Jordan et al., 1991).
- Jordan, Judith, "The Meaning of Mutuality."
- Harjo, Joy. *Poet Warrior, a Memoir*, 186.

- Vaughan, F.E., *Awakening Intuition*, 4.
- Meade, Michael, *Fate and Destiny*, 154.
- Azarova, Theresa, *A Mindful Inquiry*.
- Cohen, Gene, *The Mature Mind*, 176.
- Hollis, James, *Living an Examined Life*, 47.

Chapter Five

- Wikman, Monika, interview with Dr. Dave on Shrink Rap Radio.
- Wikman, Monika, personal interview, February 2022.
- Wikman, Monika, unpub, "At the Well of Remembrance with Ralph Metzner."
- Wikman, Monika, personal interview, March 4, 2022.

Chapter Six

- Wheelwright, Jane Hollister and Linda Wheelwright Schmidt, *The Long Shore*, 54.
- Wheelwright, Jane Hollister and Linda Wheelwright Schmidt, *The Long Shore*, 62.
- Wheelwright, Jane Hollister and Linda Wheelwright Schmidt, *The Long Shore*, 129.

- Wheelwright, Jane Hollister and Linda Wheelwright Schmidt, *The Long Shore*, 62.
- Wheelwright, Jane Hollister and Linda Wheelwright Schmidt, *The Long Shore*, 186.

Chapter Seven

- Susan, personal interview, March 9, 2022.
- Vaux, Diane Ritchey, "Helen Bonny as a musician." *Voices*, 3.
- Vaux, Diane Ritchey, "Helen Bonny as a musician." *Voices*, 4.

Chapter Eight

- Rachel, personal interview, April 3, 2022.
- Rachel, personal interview, August 5, 2022.
- Seager, Stephen B., MD, *Street Crazy*, 108.
- Rachel, email with author, April 7, 2022.
- Rachel, personal interview.
- Rachel, personal interview, April 5, 2022.
- Rachel, email with author, April 3, 2022.

Chapter Nine

- Kaye, Robbie, personal interview, March 28, 2022.
- Kaye, Robbie, *Beauty and Wisdom*, 51.

Chapter Ten

- Jillian, personal interview.
- Ferguson, Kent, personal conversation with author, May 4, 2022.
- Carroll, Lee & Jan Tober, *The Indigo Children*, 10.
- Carroll, Lee & Jan Tober, *The Indigo Children*, 112.
- Jillian, personal interview, May 2022.

Chapter 11

- Peterson, Dale, *The Woman Who Redefined Man*, xi.
- Peterson, Dale, *The Woman Who Redefined Man*, 21.
- Goodall, Jane, interview with Steve Paulson for Salon.
- Peterson, Dale, *The Woman Who Redefined Man*, 612.
- Peterson, Dale, *The Woman Who Redefined Man*, 540.
- Peterson, Dale, *The Woman Who Redefined Man*, 692.
- Goodall, Jane and Douglas Abrams. *The Book of Hope*, 204.
- Goodall, Jane and Douglas Abrams. *The Book of Hope*, 232.

Chapter Twelve

- Tornstam, Lars, *Gerotranscendence*.
- Tornstam, Lars, *Gerotranscendence*, 41.
- Tornstam, Lars, *Gerotranscendence*, 71.
- Dass, Ram and Mirabai Bush, *Walking Each Other Home*, 132.
- Tornstam, Lars, *Gerotranscendence*, 75.
- Tornstam, Lars, *Gerotranscendence*, 72.
- Robinson, John, *Mystical Activism*, 81.
- Robinson, John, *Mystical Activism*, 2.
- Robinson, John, *Mystical Activism*, 89.
- Robinson, John, *Mystical Activism*, 103.
- Dass, Ram with Rameshwar Das, *The Polishing Mirror*, 65.
- Dass, Ram with Rameshwar Das, *The Polishing Mirror*, 112.
- Dass, Ram and Mirabai Bush, *Walking Each Other Home*, 77.
- Goodall, Jane, quotes from Everyday Power website.
- Dass, Ram, *Polishing the Mirror*, 70.

References

Arrien, Angeles, *The Second Half of Life: Opening the Eight Gates of Wisdom.* Sounds True, 2007.

Azarova, Theresa, *A Mindful Inquiry into the Meaning of Individual Inspiration in a Period of Personal Challenge*, Santa Barbara, CA: Fielding diss, 2021.

Baker, Willa Blythe, *The Wakeful Body; Somatic Mindfulness as a Path to Freedom.* Shambala Pub., 2021.

Bolen, Jean Shinoda, *Crossing to Avalon, A Woman's Midlife Quest for the Sacred Feminine.* HarperCollins, 1994.

Bolton, Anthony and Randy Morris, eds, *Rites of Passage into Elderhood*, "Recognition Rites for Elders", Tom Pinkson, Second Journey, Pub., 2017.

Burnham, Sophy, *The Art of Intuition.* [Kindle] ed.

Carroll, Lee & Jan Tober, *The Indigo Children, the New Kids Have Arrived*. Hay House, 1999.

Clarkson, Ginger, *Spiritual Dimensions of Guided Imagery and Music*. Barcelona Publishers, 2018.

Cohen, Gene, *The Mature Mind: The Positive Power of the Aging Brain*. [Kindle] ed., Basic Books, 2008.

Dass, Ram, *Polishing the Mirror, How to Live from Your Spiritual Heart*. Sounds True, 2013.

Dass, Ram with Rameshwar Das, *The Polishing Mirror, How to Live from Your Spiritual Heart*. Sounds True, 2014.

Dass, Ram & Mirabai Bush, *Walking Each Other Home, Conversations on Living and Dying*. Sounds True, 2018.

Delehanty, Hugh, "Native American Novelist on *The Sentence* and Living 'in a Haunted Age,'" AARP Bulletin, November 5, 2021, https://www.aarp.org/entertainment/books/info-2021/louise-erdrich-interview.html.

Erikson, Erik H., & Erikson, Joan M., & Kivnick, Helen Q, *Vital Involvement in Old Age*. W.WQ. Norton & Co., 1986.

Goodall, Jane and Douglas Abrams, *The Book of Hope, A Survival Guide for Trying Times*. MacMillan Pub., 2021.

Goodall, Jane, *In the Shadow of Man*. Houghton Mifflin Harcourt, 1971.

Goodall, Jane, internet, https://everydaypower.com/Jane-Goodall-quotes.

Harjo, Joy, *Poet Warrior, a Memoir*. W.W. Norton, 2021.

Hollis, James, *Living an Examined Life, Wisdom for the Second Half of the Journey*. Sounds True, 2018.

Hollis, James, *Finding Meaning in the Second Half of Life, How to Finally, Really Grow Up.* Avery, 2006.

Jordan, Judith, "The Meaning of Mutuality", *Women's Growth in Connection, Writings from the Stone Center.* The Guilford Press, 1991.

Kaye, Robbie, *Beauty and Wisdom.* All Night Long Publishing, 2013.

Keating, Thomas, *Intimacy with God: An Introduction to Centering Prayer.* Crossroad Pub, 2009.

Keating, Thomas, *Invitation to Love, The Way of Christian Contemplation.* Bloomsbury, 2011.

Kübler-Ross, Elisabeth, *On Death and Dying: What the Dying Have to Teach Doctors, Nurses, Clergy & Their Own Families.* Scribner, 2014.

Leder, Drew, *Spiritual Passages, Embracing Life's Sacred Journey.* Putnam, 1997.

May, Gerald, *The Dark Night of the Soul: A Psychiatrist Explores the Connection between Darkness and Spiritual Growth.* HarperOne, 2003.

Meade, Michael, *Awakening the Soul.* Greenfire Press, 2018.

Meade, Michael, *Fate and Destiny, The Two Agreements of the Soul.* Greenfire Press, 2012.

Miller, Jean Baker, *Toward a New Psychology of Women*, (2nd Ed. Edition). Beacon Press. 1987.

Miller, Jean Baker and Irene Pierce Stiver, *The Healing Connection, How Women Form Relationships in Therapy and in Life.* Beacon Press, 2015.

Moody, Harry R., and David Carroll, *Five Stages of the Soul.* Anchor Books, 1997.

Paulson, Steve, "Jane Goodall's Animal Planet," Salon, https://www.salon.com/2009/04/14/jane_goodall/, March 17, 2022.

Peers, E. Allison, trans, & ed, *Interior Castle, St Teresa of Avila.* Doubleday, 1961.

Pinkson, Tom, *Fruitful Aging, Finding the Gold in the Golden Years*. 48HrBks, 2012.

Peterson, Dale, *The Woman Who Redefined Man*. Houghton Mifflin, 2006.

Robinson, John, *Mystical Activism: Transforming a World in Crisis*. Changemakers Books, 2020.

Sadler-Smith, Eugene, *Inside Intuition*. Routledge, 2008.

Schmidt, Lynda W., *Time Out of Mind, Trekking the Hindu Kush*. TBW Books, 1979.

Seager, Stephen B., MD, *Street Crazy, America's Mental Health Tragedy*, Westcom Press, 2009.

Thomas, William H., *What Are Old People For? How Elders Will Save the World*. VanderWyk & Burnham, 2007.

Tornstam, Lars, *Gerotranscendence, A Developmental Theory of Positive Aging*. Springer Publishing Co, 2005.

Vaillant, George E., *Aging Well: Surprising Guideposts to a Happier Life from the Landmark Study of Adult Development*. Little, Brown Spark, 2008.

Vaughan, F.E., *Awakening Intuition*. Doubleday, 1979.

Vaux, Diane Ritchey. "Helen Bonny as a Musician." *Voices: A World Forum for Music Therapy*. Vol. 10. No. 3. 2101.

Vogt, Eric, trans, *The Complete Poetry of St. Teresa of Avila. A Bilingual Edition*. University Press of the South, 2015.

Wheelwright, Jane Hollister and Linda Wheelwright Schmidt, *The Long Shore, A Psychological Experience of the Wilderness*. Sierra Club Nature and Natural Philosophy Library, 1991.

Wheelwright Schmidt, Lynda. *Time Out of Mind, Trekking the Hindu Kush*. Tbw Books, 1979.

Wikman, Monika, *Pregnant Darkness, Alchemy and the Rebirth of Consciousness*. Nicolas-Hays Inc, 2004.

Wikman, Monika, "At the Well of Remembrance with Ralph Metzner", unpub.

Zweig, Connie, *The Inner Work of Age, Shifting from Role to Soul*. Park Street Press, 2021.

PHOTOS

Photos courtesy of Tim Hauf unless otherwise noted.

Cover and Title Page

Yuksom - Dzongri - Gochala trek. Rhododendron along trekking route to Kangchenjunga's East Base Camp in Sikkim, India

Copyright page

Anna's Hummingbird, California

Table of Contents

Dew-covered wildflower along Booth Falls trail, Vail, Colorado

Author's note

Tulips, Skagit Valley, Washington

Page 2

Common Dolphins, Santa Barbara Channel, California

Page 6

Turbulent ocean near Cape Town, South Africa

Page 12 and 20

Sunflower, Great Sand Hills, Saskatchewan, Canada

Page 22

Drifting sand, Henties Bay, Namibia

Page 36

Giraffe, Namibia

Page 38 and 48

Kelso Dunes, Mojave National Preserve, California

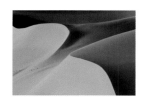

Page 50 and 60

Snowy owl at Damon Point, Ocean Shores, Washington

Page 59

Frost-covered tree branches, North Dakota

Page 62

Tunnel, Spruce Railroad trail, Olympic National Park, Washington

Page 72

Ocean waves near Dassin Island Lighthouse, South Africa

Page 74 and 82

Jannu Base Camp. Kumbhakarna (Jannu) Glacier and peak, Kangchenjunga trek, Nepal

Page 81

Trumpeter Swans, Skagit Valley, Washington

Page 84

Burchell's zebra, South Africa

Page 118

The beautiful organ pipes are a fascinating geological formation located near Twyfelfontein, Namibia

Page 128

Burchell's Zebra, Etosha National Park, Namibia

Page 130

Chimpanze, Photo 161559396 / Chimpanze © Dikkyoesin / Dreamstime.com

Page 138

Western Gull chick, Anacapa Island, Channel Islands National Park, California

Page 140

Great Blue Heron, Washington

PHOTOS

Page 149

Summertime wildflowers along the Ridge Route trail on Vail Mountain, Colorado

Page 150

Daisies, Booth Falls trail, Vail, Colorado

Page 152

Rainbow following a late-afternoon thunderstorm near the Olifantsrus restcamp, Etosha National Park, Namibia

Page 157

Wildflower, Grand Escape trail, Vail, Colorado

Page 158

Devil's Punchbowl, Lake Crescent, Olympic National Park, Washington

Page 170

Boulder Falls trail, Mt. Baker/Snoqualmie National Forest, Washington